Ninja Foodi Coo UK Edition 2024

365 days of Quick, Healthy and Delicious Recipes to Grill, Air Fry and Dehydrate. UK Measurements Added.

Dave Carter

Table of Contents

Introduction 7
Chapter 1. Overview of Ninja Foodi Features 8
Chapter 2. Getting Started with Ninja Foodi 11
   Understanding Your Ninja Foodi Appliance 11
   Essential Tools and Accessories 12
Chapter 1.   Breakfast 14
   1. Oats Granola 14
   2. Pumpkin Porridge 14
   3. Quinoa Porridge 15
   4. Dried Fruit Oatmeal 16
   5. Eggs in Avocado Cups 16
   6. Spinach & Turkey Cups 17
   7. Chicken Omelet 18
   8. Sausage & Bell Pepper Frittata 18
   9. Eggs with Tomatoes 19
   10. Banana Bread 20
   11. Grilled French toast 21
   12. Bruschetta Portobello Mushrooms 22
   13. Sausage Mixed Grill 23
   14. Sausage and Egg Loaded Breakfast Pockets 23
   15. Grilled Cinnamon Toast with Berries and Whipped Cream 24
   16. Avocado Eggs 26
   17. Coconut French toast 26
   18. Bacon-Herb Grit 27
Chapter 3. Appetizers and Snacks 28
   19. Crispy Air Fryer Chicken Wings 28
   20. Zesty Potato Skins 28
   21. Cheesy Stuffed Mushrooms 29
   22. Crispy Onion Rings 30
   23. Garlic Parmesan Sweet Potato Fries 30

24.	Buffalo Cauliflower Bites	31
25.	Mozzarella Sticks	32
26.	Crispy Tofu Bites	32
27.	Loaded Nachos	33
28.	Bacon-Wrapped Dates	34
29.	Jalapeno Poppers	34
30.	Grilled Honey Carrots	35
31.	Oregano Squash Dish	36
32.	Cajuned Eggplant Appetizer	36

Chapter 4. Soups and Stews 38

33.	Classic Chicken Noodle Soup	38
34.	Creamy Butternut Squash Soup	38
35.	Hearty Beef Stew	39
36.	Lentil and Vegetable Soup	40
37.	Thai Coconut Curry Soup	41
38.	Tomato Basil Soup	42
39.	Potato Leek Soup	42
40.	Minestrone Soup	43
41.	Chicken Tortilla Soup	44
42.	Creamy Mushroom Soup	45
43.	Corn Chowder	46
44.	Italian Soup	46
45.	Spicy Pumpkin Soup	47
46.	Broccoli Cheddar Soup	48
47.	Cajun Shrimp Skewers	49
48.	Crispy Garlic Parmesan Chicken Wings	49
49.	Zucchini Fries	50
50.	Buffalo Cauliflower Bites	51
51.	Sweet Potato Fries	51
52.	Avocado Fries	52
53.	Garlic Herb Potato Wedges	53
54.	Onion Rings	53

| 55. | Mozzarella Sticks | 54 |
| 56. | Jalapeno Poppers | 55 |

Chapter 5. Main Courses 56

57.	Teriyaki Salmon Fillets	56
58.	Mushroom Risotto	56
59.	Beef Stir Fry with Vegetables	57
60.	Shrimp Scampi	58
61.	Vegetable Lasagna	59
62.	Honey Garlic Glazed Ham	59
63.	Lemon Butter Cod	60
64.	Beef and Broccoli	61
65.	Chicken Fajitas	62
66.	Spinach and Ricotta Stuffed Chicken Breast	62
67.	Coconut Curry Chicken	63
68.	Beef Stroganoff	64
69.	Jambalaya	65
70.	Mediterranean Quinoa Salad	66
71.	Sausage and Peppers	66
72.	Teriyaki Chicken and Vegetables	67
73.	Lemon Garlic Shrimp Pasta	68

Chapter 6. One-Pot Meals 69

74.	Creamy Tuscan Chicken	69
75.	Spicy Sausage and Rice Skillet	69
76.	BBQ Chicken and Potatoes	70
77.	Lemon Garlic Shrimp Scampi	71
78.	Beef and Vegetable Stir Fry	71
79.	Creamy Tuscan Chicken Pasta	72
80.	Veggie-Packed Fried Rice	73
81.	Italian Sausage and Tortellini Soup	74
82.	Chicken and Broccoli Rice Casserole	74
83.	Lemon Garlic Butter Shrimp and Asparagus	75
84.	Creamy Mushroom Risotto	76

- 85. Beef and Vegetable Stir Fry 77
- 86. Creamy Tuscan Chicken Pasta 77
- 87. Veggie-Packed Fried Rice 78
- 88. Italian Sausage and Tortellini Soup 79
- 89. Chicken and Broccoli Rice Casserole 80
- 90. Lemon Garlic Butter Shrimp and Asparagus 80

Chapter 7. Desserts 82
- 91. Decadent Chocolate Lava Cake 82
- 92. Apple Crisp 82
- 93. Vanilla Bean Cheesecake 83
- 94. Mixed Berry Cobbler 84
- 95. Cinnamon Sugar Donuts 85
- 96. Classic Tiramisu 85
- 97. Lemon Bars 86
- 98. Chocolate Chip Cookies 87
- 99. Blueberry Pie 87
- 100. Raspberry Swirl Brownies 88
- 101. Peach Crumble 89
- 102. Key Lime Pie 90
- 103. Banoffee Pie 90
- 104. Red Velvet Cupcakes 91
- 105. Chocolate Covered Strawberries 92
- 106. Strawberry Shortcake 93
- 107. Chocolate Mousse 93
- 108. Lemon Meringue Pie 94

Chapter 8. Homemade Sauces and Dips 96
- 109. Classic Marinara Sauce 96
- 110. Creamy Garlic Aioli 96
- 111. Tangy Barbecue Sauce 97
- 112. Chunky Salsa 98
- 113. Honey Mustard Dip 98
- 114. Basil Pesto 99

115.	Chunky Salsa	99
116.	Honey Mustard Dip	100
117.	Basil Pesto	101
118.	Teriyaki Sauce	101
119.	Ranch Dressing	102
120.	Guacamole	102
Conclusion		104

Introduction

Explore the boundless world of the Ninja Foodi with this Cookbook! Say goodbye to wasted time and money in the kitchen while preparing your favorite dishes. With the Ninja Foodi, you'll whip up nutritious and delicious recipes in a flash, revolutionizing your culinary experience. It's the ultimate multitasking marvel that every kitchen deserves!

This guide is your indispensable companion on your Ninja Foodi journey, unveiling a treasure trove of tantalizing recipes from around the globe. Whether you crave spicy sensations or wholesome delights, you'll find them all here, meticulously crafted to save you precious time. With the Ninja Foodi, you can effortlessly prepare 10-15 mouthwatering dishes in record time, perfect for busy weeknights or entertaining guests. Prepare to fall head over heels for the culinary magic of the Ninja Foodi!

For many, fried food is the ultimate comfort indulgence, but the guilt of consuming greasy delights often lingers. Enter air fryers, the saviors of guilt-free frying. These innovative kitchen gadgets offer the crispy goodness of fried treats without the excess oil and calories. By harnessing the power of circulating hot air, air fryers cook food to crispy perfection using a fraction of the oil required by traditional frying methods.

In a world grappling with the health consequences of oily indulgences, air fryers emerge as champions of wellness, offering a healthier alternative to traditional frying. Their ability to reduce fat and calorie intake while preserving flavor and texture makes them a godsend for those striving for a healthier lifestyle. Whether you're looking to shed pounds or simply make smarter dietary choices, incorporating an air fryer into your kitchen arsenal is a deliciously wise decision. Say hello to guilt-free frying and embrace a healthier, happier you!

Chapter 1.   Overview of Ninja Foodi Features

In the world of kitchen appliances, the Ninja Foodi stands out as a multifunctional powerhouse, combining several cooking methods into one convenient device. With its versatility and efficiency, the Ninja Foodi has become a favorite among home cooks looking to streamline their cooking process and create delicious meals with ease. Let's delve into the myriad features that make the Ninja Foodi a must-have addition to any kitchen arsenal.

1. Pressure Cooking

One of the standout features of the Ninja Foodi is its pressure cooking capability. This function allows you to cook food quickly and efficiently by using steam pressure to raise the boiling point of water. Whether you're whipping up a batch of tender meats, hearty stews, or flavorful grains, the pressure cooking feature ensures that your meals are cooked to perfection in a fraction of the time it would take using traditional methods.

2. Air Frying

In addition to pressure cooking, the Ninja Foodi also functions as an air fryer, allowing you to enjoy crispy, golden-brown foods without the need for excessive oil. The air frying feature uses hot air circulation to evenly crisp and cook your favorite fried foods, from french fries and chicken wings to onion rings and mozzarella sticks. With the Ninja Foodi, you can indulge in all the flavor and crunch of fried foods with less guilt and hassle.

3. TenderCrisp Technology

One of the most innovative features of the Ninja Foodi is its TenderCrisp Technology, which combines the best of both pressure cooking and air frying to deliver perfectly cooked meals every time. With TenderCrisp, you can quickly pressure cook your ingredients to lock in flavor and moisture, then switch to the air frying function to achieve a crispy, golden exterior. This revolutionary technology ensures that your meals are tender on the inside and crispy on the outside, making it ideal for everything from succulent roasts to crispy chicken cutlets.

4. Multi-Cooking Functions

Versatility is key when it comes to the Ninja Foodi, and this appliance doesn't disappoint. In addition to pressure cooking and air frying, the Ninja Foodi offers a range of other cooking functions, including slow cooking, steaming, baking, roasting, and dehydrating. Whether you're preparing a slow-cooked chili, steaming vegetables, baking a batch of cookies, or dehydrating fruits for homemade snacks, the Ninja Foodi has you covered.

5. One-Pot Convenience

With the Ninja Foodi, you can say goodbye to juggling multiple pots and pans to prepare a meal. This all-in-one appliance allows you to sauté, sear, simmer, and steam ingredients directly in the cooking pot, minimizing cleanup and maximizing convenience. Whether you're cooking a one-pot pasta dish, a hearty soup, or a flavorful curry, the Ninja Foodi simplifies the cooking process, so you can spend less time in the kitchen and more time enjoying your meals.

6. Easy-to-Use Controls

Despite its advanced features, the Ninja Foodi is remarkably easy to use, thanks to its intuitive control panel and preset cooking functions. Whether you're a seasoned chef or a novice cook, you'll appreciate the user-friendly design of the Ninja Foodi, which allows you to adjust cooking times and temperatures with the touch of a button. With preset cooking programs for a variety of dishes, you can achieve perfect results every time, without the guesswork.

7. Space-Saving Design

In today's modern kitchens, space is often at a premium, which is why the compact design of the Ninja Foodi is so appealing. Despite its multifunctionality, the Ninja Foodi takes up minimal counter space, making it ideal for small kitchens, apartments, and RVs. With its sleek design and versatile cooking capabilities, the Ninja Foodi is sure to become a staple appliance in any home.

8. Easy Cleanup

Nobody enjoys scrubbing pots and pans after a meal, which is why the Ninja Foodi is designed for easy cleanup. The nonstick cooking pot and crisping basket are dishwasher safe, so you can simply pop them in the dishwasher for hassle-free cleaning. Additionally, the Ninja Foodi features a detachable pressure lid, which makes it easy to wipe down and keep clean after use.

In conclusion, the Ninja Foodi is a game-changer in the world of kitchen appliances, offering a wide range of features and functions to simplify and enhance your cooking experience. From pressure cooking and air frying to TenderCrisp technology and multi-cooking functions, the Ninja Foodi has everything you need to create delicious meals with ease. Whether you're a busy parent, a health-conscious cook, or a culinary enthusiast, the Ninja Foodi is sure to become your new favorite kitchen companion.

Chapter 2. Getting Started with Ninja Foodi

Understanding Your Ninja Foodi Appliance

In the realm of kitchen appliances, the Ninja Foodi stands out as a versatile powerhouse, combining the functionalities of a pressure cooker, air fryer, and more, all in one compact unit. This innovative appliance has revolutionized cooking for many households, offering efficiency, convenience, and a wide range of cooking possibilities. Whether you're a seasoned chef or a novice in the kitchen, understanding your Ninja Foodi appliance can elevate your culinary experience to new heights.

Introduction to the Ninja Foodi

The Ninja Foodi is a multifunctional kitchen appliance designed to streamline cooking processes and maximize efficiency. Its design incorporates various cooking methods, including pressure cooking, air frying, roasting, baking, and broiling, among others. This versatility allows users to prepare a diverse array of dishes with ease, from crispy chicken wings to tender pot roasts, all in significantly less time than traditional cooking methods.

Operating Your Ninja Foodi

1. Control Panel: Familiarize yourself with the control panel, which typically includes buttons for selecting cooking functions, adjusting time and temperature, and activating additional features such as crisping or searing.

2. Preheating: Depending on the cooking method, preheating may be necessary to ensure even cooking and optimal results. Refer to the user manual for specific preheating instructions for each function.

3. Cooking Times and Temperatures: Experiment with different cooking times and temperatures to achieve the desired results. Keep in mind that the Ninja Foodi generally cooks faster than conventional methods, so adjustments may be necessary.

4. Pressure Release Methods: After pressure cooking, there are two primary methods for releasing pressure: natural release and quick release. Natural release allows the pressure to dissipate gradually on its own, while quick release involves manually venting the steam.

5. Cleaning and Maintenance: Regular cleaning and maintenance are essential to keep your Ninja Foodi in optimal condition. Most components are dishwasher safe, but be sure to refer to the user manual for specific care instructions.

Tips and Tricks

1. Layering: Take advantage of the Ninja Foodi's stackable design by layering ingredients to cook multiple items simultaneously. Just be mindful of cooking times and adjust as needed.

2. Marinating and Seasoning: Enhance the flavor of your dishes by marinating meats and seasoning vegetables before cooking. This allows the flavors to penetrate and infuse throughout the cooking process.

3. Using Accessories: Explore the range of accessories available for the Ninja Foodi, such as baking pans, roasting racks, and silicone molds. These accessories expand the capabilities of the appliance and offer greater versatility in cooking.

4. Recipe Inspiration: Don't be afraid to get creative in the kitchen! Experiment with different recipes and ingredients to discover new flavor combinations and culinary delights.

5. Safety Precautions: Always prioritize safety when using your Ninja Foodi. Familiarize yourself with the appliance's safety features and guidelines to prevent accidents and ensure a seamless cooking experience.

Essential Tools and Accessories

In the realm of modern culinary innovation, the Ninja Foodi stands as a testament to convenience and versatility. As a multi-functional kitchen appliance, it seamlessly combines the functions of a pressure cooker, air fryer, and more, offering a myriad of cooking possibilities. Yet, to unlock its full potential, one must complement it with the right tools and accessories. From enhancing cooking precision to expanding culinary creativity, these essential companions elevate the Ninja Foodi experience to new heights.

1. Silicone Mitts: Safety is paramount in the kitchen, especially when dealing with high temperatures. Silicone mitts provide a secure grip and heat protection when handling hot components of the Ninja Foodi, such as the inner pot or air frying basket. Their flexible design ensures comfort and dexterity, allowing users to maneuver effortlessly while avoiding burns or accidents.

2. Steamer Basket: For those seeking healthier cooking options, a steamer basket is indispensable. Whether steaming vegetables, seafood, or dumplings, this accessory preserves nutrients and flavors

without the need for excessive oil or added fats. It fits snugly into the Ninja Foodi, enabling efficient steaming while maximizing space utilization for multi-layer cooking.

3. Extra Inner Pot: Convenience often lies in having spare parts readily available. An additional inner pot for the Ninja Foodi allows for seamless transitions between different recipes or ingredients without the hassle of washing in between. Whether preparing savory stews or sweet desserts, having a spare pot on hand ensures uninterrupted culinary creativity.

4. Grill Grate Insert: Craving the charred perfection of grilled dishes? The grill grate insert transforms the Ninja Foodi into a versatile indoor grill, imparting tantalizing grill marks and smoky flavors to meats, vegetables, and even fruits. Its non-stick surface ensures easy cleanup, making it a go-to accessory for barbecue enthusiasts year-round.

5. Dehydrating Rack: Harnessing the power of dehydration opens up a world of possibilities for preserving fruits, making jerky, or crafting homemade snacks. The dehydrating rack seamlessly integrates into the Ninja Foodi, providing ample space to lay out ingredients for even drying. With adjustable racks and precise temperature control, it enables effortless preparation of nutritious and flavorful dried foods.

6. Baking Pan: From decadent cakes to crispy pizzas, the baking pan expands the Ninja Foodi's repertoire to encompass a wide array of baked goods. Its durable construction and non-stick coating ensure consistent results and easy release, making baking a breeze. Whether whipping up sweet treats or savory delights, the baking pan unlocks endless baking potential within the Ninja Foodi.

7. Sous Vide Rack: Precision cooking enthusiasts will appreciate the sous vide rack for achieving restaurant-quality results at home. By immersing vacuum-sealed ingredients in a precisely controlled water bath, this accessory ensures tender, evenly cooked meats and vegetables every time. Compatible with the Ninja Foodi's temperature control features, it empowers users to elevate their culinary prowess with minimal effort.

8. Multi-Purpose Rack: Versatility is the hallmark of the Ninja Foodi, and the multi-purpose rack embodies this ethos. Whether used for roasting, broiling, or simply elevating ingredients for optimal air circulation, this accessory maximizes cooking space and efficiency. Its sturdy construction and adjustable design accommodate various cookware, from baking dishes to roasting pans, making it an indispensable tool for any culinary endeavor.

9. Instant-Read Thermometer: Achieving the perfect doneness is key to culinary success, and an instant-read thermometer provides the precision necessary to achieve it. Whether checking the internal temperature of meats, testing the doneness of baked goods, or ensuring safe cooking temperatures, this tool provides accurate readings in seconds, eliminating guesswork and ensuring consistent results.

Chapter 1. Breakfast

1. Oats Granola

Preparation Time: 15 minutes
Cooking Time: 2 hours 30 minutes
Servings: 16
Ingredients:

- 60g sunflower kernels
- 5 cups rolled oats
- 30g ground flax seeds
- 150g applesauce
- 30ml olive oil
- 30g unsalted butter
- 7g ground cinnamon
- 60g dates pitted and chopped finely
- 60g golden raisins

Directions:
1. Grease the pot of Ninja Foodi.
2. In the greased pot of Ninja Foodi, add sunflower kernels, rolled oats, flax seeds, applesauce, oil, butter, and cinnamon and stir to combine.
3. Close the Ninja Foodi with a crisping lid and select "Slow Cooker."
4. Set on "High" for 2½ hours.
5. Press "Start/Stop" to begin cooking.
6. Stir the mixture after every 30 minutes.
7. Open the lid and transfer the granola onto a large baking sheet.
8. Add the dates and raisins and stir to combine.
9. Set aside to cool completely before serving.
10. You can preserve this granola in an airtight container.

Nutrition: Calories: 189kcal; Fat: 10g; Carb: 27g; Protein: 4g

2. Pumpkin Porridge

Preparation Time: 15 minutes
Cooking Time: 5 hours
Servings: 8
Ingredients:

- 250ml unsweetened almond milk, divided

- 2 pounds pumpkin, peeled and cubed into ½-inch size
- 6-8 drops liquid stevia
- ½ teaspoon ground allspice
- 15g ground cinnamon
- 7g ground nutmeg
- ¼ teaspoon ground cloves
- 60g walnuts, chopped

Directions:
1. In the pot of Ninja Foodi, place 4 tablespoon of almond milk and remaining ingredients and stir to combine.
2. Close the Ninja Foodi with a crisping lid and select "Slow Cooker."
3. Set on "Low" for 4-5 hours.
4. Press "Start/Stop" to begin cooking.
5. Open the lid and stir in the remaining almond milk.
6. With a potato masher, mash the mixture completely.
7. Divide the porridge into serving bowls evenly.
8. Serve warm with the topping of walnuts.

Nutrition: Calories: 96kcal; Fat: 5g; Carb: 11g; Protein: 3g

3. Quinoa Porridge

Preparation Time: 10 minutes
Cooking Time: 1 minutes
Servings: 6

Ingredients:
- 270ml water
- 240ml fresh apple juice
- 300g uncooked quinoa, rinsed
- 15ml honey
- 1 cinnamon stick
- Pinch of salt

Directions:
1. In the pot of Ninja Foodi, add all ingredients and stir to combine well.
2. Close the Ninja Foodi with the pressure lid and place the pressure valve to "Seal" position.
3. Select "Pressure" and set to "High" for 1 minute.
4. Press "Start/Stop" to begin cooking.
5. Switch the valve to "Vent" and do a "Quick" release.
6. Open the lid, and with a fork, fluff the quinoa.

7. Serve warm.

Nutrition: Calories: 186kcal; Fat: 2g; Carb: 34g; Protein: 6g

4. Dried Fruit Oatmeal

Preparation Time: 10 minutes

Cooking Time: 8 hours

Servings: 8

Ingredients:

- 500g steel-cut oats
- 41g dried apricots, chopped
- 41g raisins
- 41g dried cherries
- 7g ground cinnamon
- 946ml milk
- 946ml water
- ¼ teaspoon liquid stevia

Directions:

1. In the pot of Ninja Foodi, place all ingredients and stir to combine.
2. Close the Ninja Foodi with a crisping lid and select "Slow Cooker."
3. Set on "Low" for 6-8 hours.
4. Press "Start/Stop" to begin cooking.
5. Open the lid and serve warm.

Nutrition: Calories: 148kcal; Fat: 3g; Carb: 24g; Protein: 5g

5. Eggs in Avocado Cups

Preparation Time: 10 minutes

Cooking Time: 12 minutes

Servings: 2

Ingredients:

- 1 avocado, halved and pitted
- Salt and ground black pepper, as required
- 2 eggs
- 15g Parmesan cheese, shredded
- 7g fresh chives, minced

Directions:

1. Arrange a greased square piece of foil in "Cook & Crisp Basket."
2. Arrange the "Cook & Crisp Basket" in the pot of Ninja Foodi.
3. Close the Ninja Foodi with a crisping lid and select "Bake/Roast."

4. Set the temperature to 198 degree C for 5 minutes.
5. Press "Start/Stop" to begin preheating.
6. Carefully scoop out about 2 teaspoons of flesh from each avocado half.
7. Crack 1 egg in each avocado half and sprinkle with salt, black pepper, and cheese.
8. After preheating, open the lid.
9. Place the avocado halves into the "Cook & Crisp Basket."
10. Close the Ninja Foodi with a crisping lid and Select "Bake/Roast."
11. Set the temperature to 198 degree C for 12 minutes.
12. Press "Start/Stop" to begin cooking.
13. Open the lid and transfer the avocado halves onto serving plates.
14. Top with Parmesan and chives and serve.

Nutrition: Calories: 278kcal; Fat: 24g; Carb: 9g; Protein: 8g

6. Spinach & Turkey Cups

Preparation Time: 15 minutes

Cooking Time: 23 minutes

Servings: 3

Ingredients:

- 15g unsalted butter
- 1 pound fresh baby spinach
- 4 eggs
- 7 ounces cooked turkey, chopped
- 28ml unsweetened almond milk
- Salt and ground black pepper, as required

Directions:

1. Select the "Sauté/Sear" setting of Ninja Foodi and place the butter into the pot.
2. Press "Start/Stop" to begin cooking and heat for about 2-3 minutes.
3. Add the spinach and cook for about 2-3 minutes or until just wilted.
4. Press "Start/Stop" to stop cooking and drain the liquid completely.
5. Transfer the spinach into a bowl and set aside to cool slightly.
6. Arrange the "Cook & Crisp Basket" in the pot of Ninja Foodi.
7. Close the Ninja Foodi with a crisping lid and select "Air Crisp."
8. Set the temperature to 179 degrees C for 5 minutes.
9. Press "Start/Stop" to begin preheating.
10. Divide the spinach into 4 greased ramekins, followed by the turkey.
11. Crack 1 egg into each ramekin and drizzle with almond milk.
12. Sprinkle with salt and black pepper.

13. After preheating, open the lid.
14. Place the ramekins into the "Cook & Crisp Basket."
15. Close the Ninja Foodi with a crisping lid and select "Air Crisp."
16. Set the temperature to 179 degrees C for 20 minutes.
17. Press "Start/Stop" to begin cooking.
18. Open the lid and serve hot.

Nutrition: Calories: 200kcal; Fat: 10g; Carb: 4g; Protein: 23g

7. Chicken Omelet

Preparation Time: 10 minutes

Cooking Time: 16 minutes

Servings: 2

Ingredients:

- 7g butter
- 1 small yellow onion, chopped
- ½ jalapeño pepper, seeded and chopped
- 3 eggs
- Salt and ground black pepper, as required
- 30g cooked chicken, shredded

Directions:
1. Select the "Sauté/Sear" setting of Ninja Foodi and place the butter into the pot.
2. Press "Start/Stop" to begin cooking and heat for about 2-3 minutes.
3. Add the onion and cook for about 4-5 minutes.
4. Add the jalapeño pepper and cook for about 1 minute.
5. Meanwhile, in a bowl, add the eggs, salt, and black pepper and beat well.
6. Press "Start/Stop" to stop cooking and stir in the chicken.
7. Top with the egg mixture evenly.
8. Close the Ninja Foodi with a crisping lid and select "Air Crisp."
9. Set the temperature to 179 degree C for 5 minutes.
10. Press "Start/Stop" to begin cooking.
11. Open the lid and transfer the omelet onto a plate.
12. Cut into equal-sized wedges and serve hot.

Nutrition: Calories: 153kcal; Fat: 9g; Carb: 4g; Protein: 13g

8. Sausage & Bell Pepper Frittata

Preparation Time: 15 minutes

Cooking Time: 18 minutes

Servings: 2

Ingredients:

- 15ml olive oil
- 1 chorizo sausage, sliced
- 300g bell peppers, seeded and chopped
- 4 large eggs
- Salt and ground black pepper, as required
- 30g feta cheese, crumbled
- 15g fresh parsley, chopped

Directions:

1. Select the "Sauté/Sear" setting of Ninja Foodi and place the butter into the pot.
2. Press "Start/Stop" to begin cooking and heat for about 2-3 minutes.
3. Add the sausage and bell peppers and cook for 6-8 minutes or until golden brown.
4. Meanwhile, in a small bowl, add the eggs, salt, and black pepper and beat well.
5. Press "Start/Stop" to stop cooking and place the eggs over the sausage mixture, followed by the cheese and parsley.
6. Close the Ninja Foodi with a crisping lid and select "Air Crisp."
7. Set the temperature to 179 degree C for 10 minutes.
8. Press "Start/Stop" to begin cooking.
9. Open the lid and transfer the frittata onto a platter.
10. Cut into equal-sized wedges and serve hot.

Nutrition: Calories: 398kcal; Fat: 31g; Carb: 8g; Protein: 22g

9. Eggs with Tomatoes

Preparation Time: 15 minutes

Cooking Time: 8 hours

Servings: 6

Ingredients:

- 15ml olive oil
- 1 medium yellow onion, chopped
- 2 garlic cloves, minced
- 1 jalapeño pepper, seeded and chopped finely
- 15g smoked paprika
- 7g ground cumin
- Salt, as required
- 1 (26-ounce) can diced tomatoes

- 6 eggs
- 30g feta cheese, crumbled

Directions:
1. Select the "Sauté/Sear" setting of Ninja Foodi and place the butter into the pot.
2. Press "Start/Stop" to begin cooking and heat for about 2-3 minutes.
3. Add the onion and cook for about 3-4 minutes.
4. Add the garlic, jalapeño, paprika, cumin, and salt and cook for about 1 minute.
5. Press "Start/Stop" to stop cooking.
6. Close the Ninja Foodi with a crisping lid and select "Slow Cooker."
7. Set on "Low" for 8 hours.
8. Press "Start/Stop" to begin cooking.
9. Open the lid and with the back of a spoon, make 6 wells in the tomato mixture.
10. Carefully crack 1 egg in each well.
11. Close the Ninja Foodi with a crisping lid and select "Slow Cooker."
12. Set on "High" for 20 minutes.
13. Press "Start/Stop" to begin cooking.
14. Open the lid and serve hot with the topping of cheese.

Nutrition: Calories: 134kcal; Fat: 8g; Carb: 8g; Protein: 8g

10. Banana Bread

Preparation Time: 10 minutes
Cooking Time: 50 minutes
Servings: 8
Ingredients:

- 500g flour
- 7g baking powder
- 60g sugar
- 60g butter, softened
- 2 eggs
- 15ml vanilla extract
- 4 bananas, peeled and mashed

Directions:
1. Grease a 7-inch springform pan.
2. In a bowl, mix flour and baking powder.
3. In another bowl, add sugar, butter, and eggs and beat until creamy.
4. Add the bananas and vanilla extract and beat until well combined.

5. Slowly add flour mixture, 1 cup at a time, and mix until smooth.
6. Place mixture into prepared loaf pan evenly.
7. In the pot of Ninja Foodi, place 1 cup of water.
8. Arrange the "Reversible Rack" in the pot of Ninja Foodi.
9. Place the pan over the "Reversible Rack."
10. Close the Ninja Foodi with the pressure lid and place the pressure valve to "Seal" position.
11. Select "Pressure" and set it to "High" for 50 minutes.
12. Press "Start/Stop" to begin cooking.
13. Switch the valve to "Vent" and do a "Quick" release.
14. Open the lid place the pan onto a wire rack to cool for about 10 minutes.
15. Carefully invert bread onto the wire rack to cool completely.
16. Cut into desired sized slices and serve.

Nutrition: Calories: 336kcal; Fat: 13g; Carb: 50g; Protein: 5g

11. Grilled French toast

Preparation Time: 10 minutes

Cooking Time: 8 minutes

Servings: 3

Ingredients:

- 3- 1-inch slices challah bread
- 2 eggs
- Juice of ½ orange
- ½ quart strawberries, quartered
- 15ml honey
- 15ml balsamic vinegar
- 7g orange zest
- 1/2 sprig fresh rosemary
- ½-teaspoon vanilla extract
- Salt to taste
- 1/4 cup heavy cream
- Fine sugar, for dusting, optional

Directions:

1. Spread a foil sheet on a working surface.
2. Add strawberries, balsamic, orange juice, rosemary, and zest.
3. Fold the foil edges to make a pocket.
4. Whisk egg with cream, honey, vanilla, and a pinch of salt.

5. Dip and soak the bread slices in this mixture and shake off the excess.
6. Prepare and preheat the Ninja Foodi Grill in the medium-temperature setting.
7. Once it is preheated, open the lid and place the bread slices and the foil packet on the grill.
8. Cover the Ninja Foodi Grill's lid and let them grill on the "Grilling Mode" for 2 minutes in batches.
9. Flip the bread slices and continue grilling for another 2 minutes.
10. Serve the bread with the strawberry mix on top.
11. Enjoy.

Nutrition: Calories: 387kcal; Fat: 6g; Carb: 37g; Protein: 14g

12. Bruschetta Portobello Mushrooms

Preparation Time: 10 minutes
Cooking Time: 8 minutes
Servings: 6
Ingredients:

- 500g cherry tomatoes cut in half
- 45g red onion, diced
- 45g fresh basil shredded
- Salt and black pepper to taste
- 60g butter
- 7g dried oregano
- 6 large Portobello Mushrooms, caps only, washed and dried

For Balsamic glaze:

- 15g brown sugar
- 1/4 cup balsamic vinegar

Directions

1. Start by preparing the balsamic glaze and take all its ingredients in a saucepan.
2. Stir cook this mixture for 8 minutes on medium heat then remove from the heat.
3. Take the mushrooms and brush them with the prepared glaze.
4. Stuff the remaining ingredients into the mushrooms.
5. Prepare and preheat the Ninja Foodi Grill in the medium-temperature setting.
6. Once it is preheated, open the lid and place the stuffed mushrooms in grill with their cap side down.
7. Cover the Ninja Foodi Grill's lid and let it grill on the "Grilling Mode" for 8 minutes.
8. Serve.

Nutrition: Calories: 331kcal; Fat: 2g; Carb: 69g; Protein: 8g

13. Sausage Mixed Grill

Preparation Time: 5 minutes

Cooking Time: 22 minutes

Servings: 4

Ingredients:

- 8 mini bell peppers
- 2 heads radicchio, each cut into 6 wedges
- Canola oil, for brushing
- Sea salt
- Freshly ground black pepper
- 6 breakfast sausage links
- 6 hot or sweet Italian sausage links

Directions

1. Insert the grill grate and close the hood. Select grill, set the temperature to max, and set the time to 22 minutes. Select start/Stop to begin preheating.
2. While the unit is preheating, brush the bell peppers and radicchio with the oil. Season with salt and black pepper.
3. When the unit beeps to signify it has preheated, place the bell peppers and radicchio on the grill grate close the hood and cook for 10 minutes, without flipping.
4. Meanwhile, poke the sausages with a fork or knife and brush them with some of the oil.
5. After 10 minutes, remove the vegetables and set aside. Decrease the temperature to low. Place the sausages on the grill grate close the hood and cook for 6 minutes.
6. Flip the sausages. Close the hood and cook for 6 minutes more. Remove the sausages from the grill grate.
7. Serve the sausages and vegetables on a large cutting board or serving tray.

Nutrition: Calories: 473kcal; Fat: 34g; Carb: 14g; Protein: 28g

14. Sausage and Egg Loaded Breakfast Pockets

Preparation Time: 15 minutes

Cooking Time: 23 minutes

Servings: 4

Ingredients:

- 1 (6-ounce) package ground breakfast sausage, crumbled
- 3 large eggs, lightly beaten
- 41g diced red bell pepper
- 41g thinly sliced scallions (green part only)

- Sea salt
- Freshly ground black pepper
- 1 (16-ounce) package pizza dough
- All-purpose flour, for dusting
- 240g shredded cheddar cheese
- 30ml canola oil

Directions

1. Select roast, set the temperature to 190°C, and set the time to 15 minutes. Select start/Stop to begin preheating.
2. When the unit beeps to signify it has preheated, place the sausage directly in the pot.
3. Close the hood, and cook for 10 minutes, checking the sausage every 2 to 3 minutes, breaking apart larger pieces with a wooden spoon.
4. After 10 minutes, pour the eggs, bell pepper, and scallions into the pot.
5. Stir to incorporate with the sausage evenly.
6. Close the hood and let the eggs cook for the remaining 5 minutes, stirring occasionally.
7. Transfer the sausage and egg mixture to a medium bowl to cool slightly. Season with salt and pepper.
8. Insert the crisper basket and close the hood.
9. Select air crisp, set the temperature to 176°C, and set the time to 8 minutes. Select start
10. Stop to begin preheating.
11. Meanwhile, divide the dough into four equal pieces.
12. Lightly dust a clean work surface with flour. Roll each piece of dough into a 5-inch round of even thickness.
13. Divide the sausage-egg mixture and cheese evenly among each round. Brush the outside edge of the dough with water.
14. Fold the dough over the filling, forming a half circle. Pinch the edges of the dough together to seal in the filling. Brush both sides of each pocket with the oil.
15. When the unit beeps to signify it has preheated, place the breakfast pockets in the basket. Close the hood and cook for 6 to 8 minutes, or until golden brown.

Nutrition: Calories: 639kcal; Fat: 40g; Carb: 50g; Protein: 24g

15. Grilled Cinnamon Toast with Berries and Whipped Cream

Preparation Time: 15 minutes

Cooking Time: 10 minutes

Servings: 4

Ingredients:

- 1 (15-ounce) can full- Fat coconut milk, refrigerated overnight

- 7g powdered sugar
- 1½ teaspoons vanilla extract, divided
- 240g halved strawberries
- 15ml maple syrup, plus more for garnish
- 15g brown sugar, divided
- 150ml lite coconut milk
- 2 large eggs
- ½ teaspoon ground cinnamon
- 30g unsalted butter, at room temperature
- 4 slices challah bread

Directions

1. Turn the chilled can of full-Fat coconut milk upside down (do not shake the can), open the bottom, and pour out the liquid coconut water.
2. Scoop the remaining solid coconut cream into a medium bowl. Using an electric hand mixer, whip the cream for 3 to 5 minutes, until soft peaks form.
3. Add the powdered sugar and ½ teaspoon of the vanilla to the coconut cream and whip it again until creamy. Place the bowl in the refrigerator.
4. Insert the grill grate and close the hood. Select grill, set the temperature to max, and set the time to 15 minutes. Select start and Stop to begin preheating.
5. While the unit is preheating, combine the strawberries with the maple syrup and toss to coat evenly. Sprinkle evenly with ½ tablespoon of the brown sugar.
6. In a large shallow bowl, whisk together the lite coconut milk, eggs, the remaining 7ml of vanilla, and cinnamon.
7. When the unit beeps to signify it has preheated, place the strawberries on the grill grate. Gently press the fruit down to maximize grill marks. Close the hood and grill for 4 minutes without flipping.
8. Meanwhile, butter each slice of bread on both sides. Place one slice in the egg mixture and let it soak for 1 minute. Flip the slice over and soak it for another minute.
9. Repeat with the remaining bread slices. Sprinkle each side of the toast with the remaining ½ tablespoon of brown sugar.
10. After 4 minutes, remove the strawberries from the grill and set aside. Decrease the temperature to high.
11. Place the bread on the grill grate close the hood and cook for 4 to 6 minutes, until golden and caramelized. Check often to ensure desired doneness.
12. Place the toast on a plate and top with the strawberries and whipped coconut cream. Drizzle with maple syrup, if desired.

Nutrition: Calories: 386kcal; Fat: 19g; Carb: 49g; Protein: 7g

16. Avocado Eggs

Preparation Time: 10 minutes

Cooking Time: 5 minutes

Servings: 2

Ingredients:

- 1 ripe avocado
- 1 pinch of barbecue rub
- 2 eggs
- Salt and pepper, to taste
- 1 red jalapeño, finely diced
- 1 tomato, chopped

Directions:
1. Slice avocado in half and remove its pit.
2. Remove some flesh from the center then crack an egg into the halves.
3. Drizzle barbecue rub, salt, pepper, jalapeno and tomato on top.
4. Prepare and preheat the Ninja Foodi Grill in a High-temperature setting.
5. Once it is preheated, open the lid and place the stuffed avocado in grill with their skin side down.
6. Cover the Ninja Foodi Grill's lid and let it grill on the "Grilling Mode" for 5 minutes.
7. Serve.

Nutrition: Calories: 322kcal; Fat: 11g; Carb: 14g; Protein: 17g

17. Coconut French toast

Preparation Time: 10 minutes

Cooking Time: 16 minutes

Servings: 5

Ingredients:

- 60ml milk
- 3 large eggs
- 1 (12-oz) loaf bread- 10 slices
- 60g sugar
- Cooking spray
- 240ml of coconut milk
- 10 (1/4-inch-thick slices pineapple, peeled
- 1/2 cup coconut flakes

Directions:
1. Whisk the coconut milk with sugar, eggs, and fat-free milk in a bowl.

2. Dip the bread in this mixture and keep it aside for 1 minute.
3. Prepare and preheat the Ninja Foodi Grill on medium-temperature setting.
4. Once it is preheated, open the lid and place 5 bread slices on the grill.
5. Cover the Ninja Foodi Grill's lid and let it grill on the "Grilling Mode" for 2 minutes.
6. Flip the slices and continue grilling for another 2 minutes.
7. Cook the remaining 5 slices in a similar way.
8. Now grill 5 pineapples slices on the grill for 2 minutes per side.
9. Grill the remaining pineapple in the same way.
10. Serve the bread with pineapple on top.
11. Garnish with coconut and serve.

Nutrition: Calories: 197kcal; Fat: 15g; Carb: 58g; Protein: 7g

18. Bacon-Herb Grit

Preparation Time: 10 minutes
Cooking Time: 10 minutes
Servings: 4
Ingredients:

- 15g minced fresh
- 15g chopped fresh parsley
- 3.5g garlic powder
- 3.5g black pepper
- 3 bacon slices, cooked and crumbled
- 120g shredded cheddar cheese
- 946ml instant grits
- Cooking spray

Directions:

1. Start by mixing the first seven ingredients in a suitable bowl.
2. Spread this mixture in a 10-inch baking pan and refrigerate for 1 hour.
3. Flip the pan on a plate and cut the grits mixture into 4 triangles.
4. Prepare and preheat the Ninja Foodi Grill in the medium-temperature setting.
5. Once it is preheated, open the lid and place the grit slices in the grill.
6. Cover the Ninja Foodi Grill's lid and let it grill on the "Grilling Mode" for 5 minutes per side.
7. Serve.

Nutrition: Calories: 138kcal; Fat: 3g; Carb: 32g; Protein: 10g

Chapter 3. Appetizers and Snacks

19. Crispy Air Fryer Chicken Wings

Preparation Time: 10 minutes
Cooking Time: 25 minutes
Servings: 4
Ingredients:

- 453g chicken wings
- 30ml olive oil
- 7g garlic powder
- 7g paprika
- Salt and pepper to taste

Directions:
1. Preheat the Ninja Foodi Air Fryer to 200°C.
2. In a bowl, toss chicken wings with olive oil, garlic powder, paprika, salt, and pepper.
3. Place the wings in the Air Fryer basket in a single layer.
4. Air fry for 20-25 minutes, flipping halfway through, until wings are crispy and cooked through.
5. Serve hot with your favorite dipping sauce.

Nutrition: Calories: 250kcal; Fat: 18g; Carb: 1g; Protein: 20g

20. Zesty Potato Skins

Preparation Time: 15 minutes
Cooking Time: 30 minutes
Servings: 6
Ingredients:

- 6 large russet potatoes
- 240g shredded cheddar cheese
- 6 slices bacon, cooked and crumbled
- 60g sour cream
- 2 green onions, chopped
- Salt and pepper to taste

Directions:

1. Scrub the potatoes thoroughly under running water to remove any dirt. Pat them dry with paper towels.
2. Pierce each potato several times with a fork to allow steam to escape during cooking.
3. Place the potatoes in the Ninja Foodi Air Fryer basket with 1 cup of water at the bottom of the cooking pot.
4. Close the lid of the Ninja Foodi and set the Air Fryer function to 200°C.
5. Air fry the potatoes for 30 minutes, or until they are fork-tender.
6. Once the potatoes are cooked, carefully remove them from the Air Fryer basket and allow them to cool slightly.
7. Cut each potato in half lengthwise and scoop out the flesh, leaving about 1/4 inch of potato attached to the skin. Save the scooped-out potato flesh for another use or discard.
8. Brush the potato skins with olive oil and season them with salt and pepper.
9. Place the potato skins back into the Air Fryer basket, skin side down.
10. Air fry the potato skins for 10 minutes at 200°C until they are crispy and golden brown.
11. Once the potato skins are crispy, remove them from the Air Fryer basket and sprinkle each skin with shredded cheese and crumbled bacon.
12. Return the loaded potato skins to the Air Fryer basket and air fry for an additional 5 minutes at 200°C, or until the cheese is melted and bubbly.
13. Carefully remove the loaded potato skins from the Ninja Foodi Air Fryer and transfer them to a serving platter.
14. Serve hot with sour cream and chopped green onions on top.

Nutrition: Calories: 280kcal; Fat: 15g; Carb: 25g; Protein: 12g

21. Cheesy Stuffed Mushrooms

Preparation Time: 20 minutes
Cooking Time: 15 minutes
Servings: 4
Ingredients:

- 12 large mushrooms, stems removed
- 120g breadcrumbs
- 120g shredded mozzarella cheese
- 60g grated Parmesan cheese
- 2 cloves garlic, minced
- 30g chopped fresh parsley
- 30ml olive oil
- Salt and pepper to taste

Directions:

1. Preheat the Ninja Foodi Air Fryer to 190°C.
2. In a bowl, mix together breadcrumbs, mozzarella cheese, Parmesan cheese, garlic, parsley, olive oil, salt, and pepper.
3. Fill each mushroom cap with the breadcrumb mixture.
4. Place stuffed mushrooms in the Air Fryer basket in a single layer.
5. Air fry for 12-15 minutes until mushrooms are tender and filling is golden brown.
6. Serve hot as an appetizer or side dish.

Nutrition: Calories: 150kcal; Fat: 9g; Carb: 12g; Protein: 6g

22. Crispy Onion Rings

Preparation Time: 15 minutes
Cooking Time: 10 minutes
Servings: 4
Ingredients:

- 2 large onions, sliced into rings
- 240g all-purpose flour
- 2 eggs, beaten
- 240g breadcrumbs
- 7g garlic powder
- 7g paprika
- Salt and pepper to taste

Directions:
1. Preheat the Ninja Foodi Air Fryer to 200°C.
2. In separate bowls, place flour, beaten eggs, and breadcrumbs mixed with garlic powder, paprika, salt, and pepper.
3. Dip each onion ring into the flour, then the beaten eggs, and finally coat with breadcrumbs.
4. Place the coated onion rings in the Air Fryer basket in a single layer.
5. Air fry for 8-10 minutes until onion rings are golden brown and crispy.
6. Serve hot with your favorite dipping sauce.

Nutrition: Calories: 200kcal; Fat: 4g; Carb: 35g; Protein: 6g

23. Garlic Parmesan Sweet Potato Fries

Preparation Time: 20 minutes
Cooking Time: 20 minutes
Servings: 4

Ingredients:

- 2 large sweet potatoes, cut into fries
- 30ml olive oil
- 60g grated Parmesan cheese
- 2 cloves garlic, minced
- 15g chopped fresh parsley
- Salt and pepper to taste

Directions:
1. Preheat the Ninja Foodi Air Fryer to 200°C.
2. In a bowl, toss sweet potato fries with olive oil, Parmesan cheese, garlic, parsley, salt, and pepper.
3. Place the seasoned sweet potato fries in the Air Fryer basket in a single layer.
4. Air fry for 18-20 minutes, shaking the basket halfway through, until fries are golden brown and crispy.
5. Serve hot as a delicious snack or side dish.

Nutrition: Calories: 180kcal; Fat: 7g; Carb: 28g; Protein: 3g

24. Buffalo Cauliflower Bites

Preparation Time: 15 minutes
Cooking Time: 20 minutes
Servings: 4

Ingredients:

- 1 head cauliflower, cut into florets
- 120g all-purpose flour
- 120ml milk
- 120g buffalo sauce
- 30ml melted butter
- 7g garlic powder
- Salt and pepper to taste

Directions:
1. Preheat the Ninja Foodi Air Fryer to 200°C.
2. In a bowl, whisk together flour, milk, garlic powder, salt, and pepper to make a batter.
3. Dip each cauliflower floret into the batter, shaking off any excess, and place them in the Air Fryer basket.
4. Air fry for 10 minutes, shaking the basket halfway through, until cauliflower is golden brown and crispy.
5. In a separate bowl, mix together buffalo sauce and melted butter.
6. Toss the cooked cauliflower in the buffalo sauce mixture until evenly coated.
7. Air fry for an additional 8-10 minutes until cauliflower is crispy and sauce is caramelized.

8. Serve hot with ranch or blue cheese dressing for dipping.

Nutrition: Calories: 150kcal; Fat: 6g; Carb: 20g; Protein: 4g

25. Mozzarella Sticks

Preparation Time: 20 minutes
Cooking Time: 10 minutes
Servings: 4
Ingredients:

- 8 mozzarella string cheese sticks
- 120g all-purpose flour
- 2 eggs, beaten
- 240g breadcrumbs
- 7g Italian seasoning
- Marinara sauce for dipping

Directions:
1. Preheat the Ninja Foodi Air Fryer to 190°C.
2. Cut each mozzarella stick in half to make 16 shorter sticks.
3. Place flour, beaten eggs, and breadcrumbs mixed with Italian seasoning in separate bowls.
4. Dip each mozzarella stick into the flour, then the beaten eggs, and finally coat with breadcrumbs.
5. Place the coated mozzarella sticks in the Air Fryer basket in a single layer.
6. Air fry for 8-10 minutes until golden brown and cheese is melted.
7. Serve hot with marinara sauce for dipping.

Nutrition: Calories: 220kcal; Fat: 10g; Carb: 18g; Protein: 14g

26. Crispy Tofu Bites

Preparation Time: 30 minutes
Cooking Time: 20 minutes
Servings: 4
Ingredients:

- 1 block firm tofu, drained and pressed
- 60g cornstarch
- 60ml soy sauce
- 30ml maple syrup
- 15ml sesame oil
- 7g garlic powder

- 7g onion powder
- 1/2 tsp smoked paprika
- 60g breadcrumbs
- 2 green onions, thinly sliced

Directions:
1. Preheat the Ninja Foodi Air Fryer to 200°C.
2. Cut pressed tofu into bite-sized cubes.
3. In a bowl, whisk together cornstarch, soy sauce, maple syrup, sesame oil, garlic powder, onion powder, and smoked paprika to make the marinade.
4. Toss tofu cubes in the marinade until evenly coated.
5. In a separate bowl, mix breadcrumbs with thinly sliced green onions.
6. Coat marinated tofu cubes with breadcrumb mixture.
7. Place coated tofu cubes in the Air Fryer basket in a single layer.
8. Air fry for 15-20 minutes, shaking the basket halfway through, until tofu is crispy and golden brown.
9. Serve hot with dipping sauce or on top of salads.

Nutrition: Calories: 180kcal; Fat: 6g; Carb: 20g; Protein: 12g

27. Loaded Nachos

Preparation Time: 15 minutes
Cooking Time: 10 minutes
Servings: 4
Ingredients:

- 1 bag tortilla chips
- 240g shredded cheddar cheese
- 240g cooked black beans
- 240g cooked ground beef or turkey
- 120g diced tomatoes
- 60g diced red onion
- 60g sliced black olives
- 60g sliced jalapenos
- 60g sour cream
- 60g guacamole
- 60g salsa
- 30g chopped fresh cilantro

Directions:
1. Preheat the Ninja Foodi Air Fryer to 200°C.
2. Spread tortilla chips in a single layer on the Air Fryer basket.

3. Sprinkle shredded cheddar cheese evenly over the tortilla chips.
4. Top with cooked black beans, ground beef or turkey, diced tomatoes, diced red onion, sliced black olives, and sliced jalapenos.
5. Air fry for 8-10 minutes until cheese is melted and bubbly.
6. Remove loaded nachos from the Air Fryer and transfer to a serving platter.
7. Serve hot with dollops of sour cream, guacamole, salsa, and chopped cilantro.

Nutrition: Calories: 350kcal; Fat: 20g; Carb: 30g; Protein: 15g

28. Bacon-Wrapped Dates

Preparation Time: 15 minutes
Cooking Time: 15 minutes
Servings: 4
Ingredients:

- 12 Medjool dates, pitted
- 6 slices bacon, cut in half
- 60g goat cheese
- 60g chopped almonds

Directions:
1. Preheat the Ninja Foodi Air Fryer to 190°C.
2. Stuff each pitted date with goat cheese and a sprinkle of chopped almonds.
3. Wrap each stuffed date with a half slice of bacon and secure with a toothpick.
4. Place the bacon-wrapped dates in the Air Fryer basket in a single layer.
5. Air fry for 12-15 minutes until bacon is crispy.
6. Remove from the Air Fryer and let cool slightly before serving.

Nutrition: Calories: 280kcal; Fat: 14g; Carb: 30g; Protein: 8g

29. Jalapeno Poppers

Preparation Time: 20 minutes
Cooking Time: 15 minutes
Servings: 4
Ingredients:

- 8 large jalapeno peppers
- 4 oz cream cheese, softened
- 120g shredded cheddar cheese
- 4 slices bacon, cooked and crumbled
- 1/4 tsp garlic powder
- 1/4 tsp onion powder

- Salt and pepper to taste
- 60g breadcrumbs
- Cooking spray

Directions:
1. Preheat the Ninja Foodi Air Fryer to 190°C.
2. Cut jalapeno peppers in half lengthwise and remove seeds and membranes.
3. In a bowl, mix together cream cheese, shredded cheddar cheese, crumbled bacon, garlic powder, onion powder, salt, and pepper until well combined.
4. Fill each jalapeno half with the cream cheese mixture.
5. Place filled jalapeno halves on a baking sheet lined with parchment paper.
6. Sprinkle breadcrumbs over the filled jalapenos.
7. Lightly spray the tops of the jalapenos with cooking spray.
8. Transfer the jalapeno poppers to the Air Fryer basket in a single layer.
9. Air fry for 12-15 minutes until jalapenos are tender and breadcrumbs are golden brown.
10. Serve hot as a spicy and cheesy appetizer.

Nutrition: Calories: 150kcal; Fat: 11g; Carb: 8g; Protein: 6g

30. Grilled Honey Carrots

Preparation Time: 15 minutes
Cooking Time: 10 minutes
Servings: 4-5

Ingredients

- 30ml melted butter
- 6 carrots, peeled, cut lengthwise
- 15g parsley, chopped
- 15g rosemary, chopped
- 15ml honey
- 7g kosher salt

Directions:
1. Take ninja foodi grill, arrange it over your kitchen platform, and open the top lid.
2. Arrange the grill grate and close the top lid.
3. Press "grill" and select the "max" grill function. Adjust the timer to 10 minutes and then press "start/Stop." Ninja foodi will start preheating.
4. Ninja foodi is preheated and ready to cook when it starts to beep. After you hear a beep, open the top lid.
5. Arrange the carrots over the grill grate.

6. Close the top lid and cook for 5 minutes. Now open the top lid, flip the carrots.
7. Close the top lid and cook for 5 more minutes.
8. Serve warm.

Nutrition: Calories: 82kcal; Fat: 4g; Carb: 5g; Protein: 0.5g

31. Oregano Squash Dish

Preparation Time: 10 minutes
Cooking Time: 16 minutes
Servings: 4
Ingredients:

- 1 medium butternut squash, peeled, seeded, and cut into ½ inch slices
- 1 and ½ teaspoons oregano, dried
- 7g thyme, dried
- 15ml olive oil
- ½ teaspoon salt
- ¼ teaspoon black pepper

Directions

1. Add slices alongside other ingredients into a mixing bowl
2. Mix them well
3. Pre-heat Ninja Foodi by pressing the "GRILL" option and setting it to "MED."
4. Set the timer to 16 minutes
5. Let it pre-heat until you hear a beep.
6. Arrange squash slices over the grill grate.
7. Cook for 8 minutes. Then flip and cook for 8 minutes more.
8. Serve and enjoy!

Nutrition: Calories: 238kcal; Fat: 12g; Carb: 36g; Protein: 15g

32. Cajuned Eggplant Appetizer

Preparation Time: 5-10 minutes
Cooking Time: 10 minutes
Servings: 4
Ingredients:

- 30ml lime juice
- 22g Cajun seasoning
- 2 small eggplants, cut into slices (1/2 inch)
- 60ml olive oil

Directions:
1. Coat the eggplant slices with the oil, lemon juice, and Cajun seasoning.
2. Take ninja foodi grill, arrange it over your kitchen platform, and open the top lid.
3. Arrange the grill grate and close the top lid.
4. Press "grill" and select the "med" grill function. Adjust the timer to 10 minutes and then press "start/Stop." Ninja foodi will start pre-heating.
5. Ninja foodi is preheated and ready to cook when it starts to beep. After you hear a beep, open the top lid.
6. Arrange the eggplant slices over the grill grate.
7. Close the top lid and cook for 5 minutes. Now open the top lid, flip the eggplant slices.
8. Close the top lid and cook for 5 more minutes.
9. Divide into serving plates.
10. Serve warm

Nutrition: Calories: 362kcal; Fat: 11g; Carb: 16g; Protein: 8g

Chapter 4. Soups and Stews

33. Classic Chicken Noodle Soup

Preparation Time: 15 minutes
Cooking Time: 30 minutes
Servings: 6
Ingredients:

- 15ml olive oil
- 1 onion, diced
- 2 carrots, sliced
- 2 celery stalks, sliced
- 2 cloves garlic, minced
- 6 cups chicken broth
- 500g shredded cooked chicken
- 500g egg noodles
- Salt and pepper to taste
- Fresh parsley, chopped (for garnish)

Directions:
1. Preheat the Ninja Foodi Air Fryer to 200°C using the Air Crisp function.
2. In the inner pot, add olive oil, onion, carrots, and celery. Air crisp for 5 minutes until vegetables are slightly softened.
3. Add minced garlic and air crisp for an additional minute.
4. Pour in chicken broth and shredded chicken. Close the lid and set the pressure release valve to SEAL. Pressure cook on HIGH for 10 minutes.
5. Once done, quick release the pressure and carefully open the lid.
6. Switch to the Air Crisp function again and add egg noodles to the soup. Air crisp for 8-10 minutes until noodles are tender.
7. Season with salt and pepper to taste.
8. Serve hot, garnished with chopped fresh parsley.

Nutrition: Calories: 250kcal; Fat: 7g; Carb: 26g; Protein: 18g

34. Creamy Butternut Squash Soup

Preparation Time: 20 minutes
Cooking Time: 30 minutes
Servings: 6
Ingredients:

- 1 butternut squash, peeled, seeded, and cubed
- 1 onion, chopped
- 2 carrots, chopped
- 2 cloves garlic, minced
- 946ml vegetable broth
- 240ml coconut milk
- 7g ground cinnamon
- Salt and pepper to taste

Directions:
1. Preheat the Ninja Foodi Air Fryer to 200°C using the Air Roast function.
2. Place cubed butternut squash, chopped onion, carrots, and minced garlic in the air fryer basket.
3. Air roast for 15-20 minutes until the vegetables are tender and slightly caramelized.
4. Transfer the roasted vegetables to the Ninja Foodi Pressure Cooker.
5. Add vegetable broth, coconut milk, and ground cinnamon to the pressure cooker.
6. Close the lid and set the pressure release valve to SEAL. Pressure cook on HIGH for 10 minutes.
7. Once done, quick release the pressure and carefully open the lid.
8. Use an immersion blender to puree the soup until smooth.
9. Season with salt and pepper to taste.
10. Serve hot, optionally garnished with a drizzle of coconut milk and a sprinkle of ground cinnamon.

Nutrition: Calories: 180kcal; Fat: 8g; Carb: 27g; Protein: 3g

35. Hearty Beef Stew

Preparation Time: 20 minutes
Cooking Time: 1 hour
Servings: 6
Ingredients:

- 1.5 lbs beef stew meat, cubed
- 30ml olive oil
- 1 onion, chopped
- 2 carrots, sliced
- 2 celery stalks, sliced
- 2 cloves garlic, minced

- 946ml beef broth
- 240ml red wine (optional)
- 2 potatoes, peeled and cubed
- 240g frozen peas
- 30g tomato paste
- 7g dried thyme
- Salt and pepper to taste

Directions:
1. Preheat the Ninja Foodi Pressure Cooker on the SEAR/SAUTÉ function.
2. Add olive oil and brown beef stew meat in batches. Remove and set aside.
3. In the same pot, sauté onion, carrots, celery, and garlic until softened.
4. Return browned beef to the pot. Add beef broth, red wine (if using), potatoes, frozen peas, tomato paste, and dried thyme.
5. Close the lid and set the pressure release valve to SEAL. Pressure cook on HIGH for 40 minutes.
6. Once done, quick release the pressure and carefully open the lid.
7. Season with salt and pepper to taste.
8. Serve hot.

Nutrition: Calories: 350kcal; Fat: 12g; Carb: 25g; Protein: 25g

36. Lentil and Vegetable Soup

Preparation Time: 15 minutes
Cooking Time: 30 minutes
Servings: 6
Ingredients:

- 240g dried lentils, rinsed and drained
- 946ml vegetable broth
- 1 onion, chopped
- 2 carrots, chopped
- 2 celery stalks, chopped
- 2 cloves garlic, minced
- 1 can (14 oz) diced tomatoes
- 7g ground cumin
- 7g ground coriander
- 1 bay leaf
- Salt and pepper to taste
- Fresh parsley, chopped (for garnish)

Directions:
1. Preheat the Ninja Foodi Pressure Cooker on the SAUTÉ function.
2. Add chopped onion, carrots, celery, and garlic. Sauté until softened.
3. Stir in dried lentils, vegetable broth, diced tomatoes, ground cumin, ground coriander, and bay leaf.
4. Close the lid and set the pressure release valve to SEAL. Pressure cook on HIGH for 15 minutes.
5. Once done, quick release the pressure and carefully open the lid.
6. Discard the bay leaf and season with salt and pepper to taste.
7. Serve hot, garnished with chopped fresh parsley.

Nutrition: Calories: 220kcal; Fat: 1g; Carb: 40g; Protein: 14g

37. Thai Coconut Curry Soup

Preparation Time: 20 minutes
Cooking Time: 30 minutes
Servings: 4
Ingredients:

- 15ml olive oil
- 1 onion, chopped
- 2 carrots, sliced
- 2 cloves garlic, minced
- 30g Thai red curry paste
- 946ml chicken broth
- 1 can (14 oz) coconut milk
- 15ml fish sauce
- 15g brown sugar
- 240g sliced mushrooms
- 1 bell pepper, sliced
- 240g cooked chicken, shredded
- Juice of 1 lime
- Fresh cilantro, chopped (for garnish)

Directions:
1. Preheat the Ninja Foodi Pressure Cooker on the SAUTÉ function.
2. Add olive oil, chopped onion, carrots, and minced garlic. Sauté until softened.
3. Stir in Thai red curry paste and cook for another minute.
4. Pour in chicken broth, coconut milk, fish sauce, and brown sugar. Stir to combine.
5. Add sliced mushrooms, bell pepper, and shredded chicken to the pot.
6. Close the lid and set the pressure release valve to SEAL. Pressure cook on HIGH for 10 minutes.
7. Once done, quick release the pressure and carefully open the lid.

8. Stir in lime juice.
9. Serve hot, garnished with chopped fresh cilantro.

Nutrition: Calories: 350kcal; Fat: 25g; Carb: 20g; Protein: 15g

38. Tomato Basil Soup

Preparation Time: 15 minutes
Cooking Time: 30 minutes
Servings: 4
Ingredients:

- 30ml olive oil
- 1 onion, chopped
- 2 cloves garlic, minced
- 2 cans (14 oz each) diced tomatoes
- 500ml vegetable broth
- 7g sugar
- Salt and pepper to taste
- 60g chopped fresh basil
- 60g heavy cream (optional)
- Grated Parmesan cheese (for garnish)

Directions:
1. Preheat the Ninja Foodi Pressure Cooker on the SAUTÉ function.
2. Add olive oil, chopped onion, and minced garlic. Sauté until softened.
3. Stir in diced tomatoes (with their juices), vegetable broth, and sugar.
4. Close the lid and set the pressure release valve to SEAL. Pressure cook on HIGH for 15 minutes.
5. Once done, quick release the pressure and carefully open the lid.
6. Use an immersion blender to puree the soup until smooth.
7. Stir in chopped fresh basil and heavy cream (if using).
8. Season with salt and pepper to taste.
9. Serve hot, garnished with grated Parmesan cheese.

Nutrition: Calories: 200kcal; Fat: 14g; Carb: 18g; Protein: 4g

39. Potato Leek Soup

Preparation Time: 15 minutes
Cooking Time: 30 minutes
Servings: 4
Ingredients:

- 30g butter

- 2 leeks, white and light green parts only, thinly sliced
- 2 cloves garlic, minced
- 2 potatoes, peeled and diced
- 946ml chicken broth
- 1 bay leaf
- Salt and pepper to taste
- 120g heavy cream
- Chopped chives (for garnish)

Directions:
1. Preheat the Ninja Foodi Pressure Cooker on the SAUTÉ function.
2. Add butter, sliced leeks, and minced garlic. Sauté until softened.
3. Stir in diced potatoes, chicken broth, and bay leaf.
4. Close the lid and set the pressure release valve to SEAL. Pressure cook on HIGH for 10 minutes.
5. Once done, quick release the pressure and carefully open the lid.
6. Remove the bay leaf and use an immersion blender to puree the soup until smooth.
7. Stir in heavy cream and season with salt and pepper to taste.
8. Serve hot, garnished with chopped chives.

Nutrition: Calories: 250kcal; Fat: 15g; Carb: 25g; Protein: 4g

40. Minestrone Soup

Preparation Time: 20 minutes
Cooking Time: 30 minutes
Servings: 6
Ingredients:

- 30ml olive oil
- 1 onion, chopped
- 2 carrots, diced
- 2 celery stalks, diced
- 2 cloves garlic, minced
- 1 zucchini, diced
- 240g green beans, cut into 1-inch pieces
- 1 can (14 oz) diced tomatoes
- 6 cups vegetable broth
- 7g dried thyme
- 7g dried oregano
- 240g cooked small pasta (such as ditalini or macaroni)
- Salt and pepper to taste

- Grated Parmesan cheese (for garnish)

Directions:
1. Preheat the Ninja Foodi Pressure Cooker on the SAUTÉ function.
2. Add olive oil, chopped onion, carrots, celery, and minced garlic. Sauté until softened.
3. Stir in diced zucchini, green beans, diced tomatoes (with their juices), vegetable broth, dried thyme, and dried oregano.
4. Close the lid and set the pressure release valve to SEAL. Pressure cook on HIGH for 10 minutes.
5. Once done, quick release the pressure and carefully open the lid.
6. Stir in cooked pasta and season with salt and pepper to taste.
7. Serve hot, garnished with grated Parmesan cheese.

Nutrition: Calories: 200kcal; Fat: 5g; Carb: 30g; Protein: 6g

41. Chicken Tortilla Soup

Preparation Time: 15 minutes
Cooking Time: 30 minutes
Servings: 4
Ingredients:

- 15ml olive oil
- 1 onion, diced
- 2 cloves garlic, minced
- 1 jalapeno, seeded and chopped
- 1 red bell pepper, diced
- 1 can (14 oz) diced tomatoes
- 946ml chicken broth
- 7g ground cumin
- 7g chili powder
- 7g smoked paprika
- 500g cooked shredded chicken
- 240g frozen corn kernels
- 240g black beans, drained and rinsed
- Salt and pepper to taste
- Tortilla strips, avocado slices, chopped cilantro (for garnish)

Directions:
1. Preheat the Ninja Foodi Pressure Cooker on the SAUTÉ function.
2. Add olive oil, diced onion, minced garlic, chopped jalapeno, and diced red bell pepper. Sauté until softened.

3. Stir in diced tomatoes (with their juices), chicken broth, ground cumin, chili powder, and smoked paprika.
4. Close the lid and set the pressure release valve to SEAL. Pressure cook on HIGH for 10 minutes.
5. Once done, quick release the pressure and carefully open the lid.
6. Stir in shredded chicken, frozen corn kernels, and black beans.
7. Season with salt and pepper to taste.
8. Serve hot, garnished with tortilla strips, avocado slices, and chopped cilantro.

Nutrition: Calories: 280kcal; Fat: 8g; Carb: 30g; Protein: 20g

42. Creamy Mushroom Soup

Preparation Time: 15 minutes
Cooking Time: 30 minutes
Servings: 4
Ingredients:

- 30g butter
- 1 onion, chopped
- 2 cloves garlic, minced
- 453g mushrooms, sliced
- 946ml vegetable broth
- 240g heavy cream
- 30g all-purpose flour
- Salt and pepper to taste
- Chopped fresh parsley (for garnish)

Directions:
1. Preheat the Ninja Foodi Pressure Cooker on the SAUTÉ function.
2. Add butter, chopped onion, and minced garlic. Sauté until softened.
3. Add sliced mushrooms and cook until they release their moisture and start to brown.
4. Stir in vegetable broth and bring to a simmer.
5. In a small bowl, whisk together heavy cream and all-purpose flour until smooth. Pour into the soup and stir well.
6. Close the lid and set the pressure release valve to SEAL. Pressure cook on HIGH for 10 minutes.
7. Once done, quick release the pressure and carefully open the lid.
8. Season with salt and pepper to taste.
9. Serve hot, garnished with chopped fresh parsley.

Nutrition: Calories: 320kcal; Fat: 25g; Carb: 20g; Protein: 6g

43. Corn Chowder

Preparation Time: 20 minutes
Cooking Time: 30 minutes
Servings: 4
Ingredients:

- 4 slices bacon, chopped
- 1 onion, diced
- 2 cloves garlic, minced
- 2 potatoes, peeled and diced
- 500g frozen corn kernels
- 946ml chicken broth
- 240g heavy cream
- 30g all-purpose flour
- Salt and pepper to taste
- Chopped green onions (for garnish)

Directions:
1. Preheat the Ninja Foodi Pressure Cooker on the SAUTÉ function.
2. Add chopped bacon and cook until crispy. Remove bacon and set aside.
3. In the bacon drippings, sauté diced onion and minced garlic until softened.
4. Add diced potatoes, frozen corn kernels, and chicken broth to the pot. Bring to a simmer.
5. In a small bowl, whisk together heavy cream and all-purpose flour until smooth. Pour into the soup and stir well.
6. Close the lid and set the pressure release valve to SEAL. Pressure cook on HIGH for 10 minutes.
7. Once done, quick release the pressure and carefully open the lid.
8. Season with salt and pepper to taste.
9. Serve hot, garnished with chopped green onions and crispy bacon.

Nutrition: Calories: 380kcal; Fat: 25g; Carb: 30g; Protein: 8g

44. Italian Soup

Preparation Time: 20 minutes
Cooking Time: 30 minutes
Servings: 6
Ingredients:

- 15ml olive oil
- 1 onion, finely chopped
- 2 carrots, diced

- 2 stalks celery, diced
- 2 cloves garlic, minced
- 6 cups chicken broth
- 240g acini di pepe pasta (or any small pasta)
- 8 oz ground beef
- 1 egg, lightly beaten
- 60g breadcrumbs
- 30g grated Parmesan cheese
- 500g fresh spinach, chopped
- Salt and pepper to taste
- Fresh parsley, chopped (for garnish)

Directions:
1. Preheat the Ninja Foodi Air Fryer to 190°C using the Air Roast function.
2. In a bowl, mix together ground beef, egg, breadcrumbs, grated Parmesan cheese, salt, and pepper. Form into small meatballs.
3. Place meatballs on the Air Fryer basket in a single layer. Air roast for 10-12 minutes until browned and cooked through.
4. In the inner pot of the Ninja Foodi Pressure Cooker, heat olive oil using the SAUTÉ function.
5. Add chopped onion, diced carrots, diced celery, and minced garlic. Sauté until vegetables are softened.
6. Pour in chicken broth and bring to a simmer.
7. Stir in acini di pepe pasta and chopped spinach.
8. Close the lid and set the pressure release valve to SEAL. Pressure cook on HIGH for 5 minutes.
9. Once done, quick release the pressure and carefully open the lid.
10. Stir in cooked meatballs.
11. Season with salt and pepper to taste.
12. Serve hot, garnished with chopped fresh parsley.

Nutrition: Calories: 280kcal; Fat: 10g; Carb: 25g; Protein: 18g

45. Spicy Pumpkin Soup

Preparation Time: 15 minutes
Cooking Time: 30 minutes
Servings: 4
Ingredients:

- 15ml olive oil
- 1 onion, chopped
- 2 cloves garlic, minced
- 7g ground cumin

- 3.5g ground cinnamon
- 1.42g ground nutmeg
- 1.42g cayenne pepper
- 500g pumpkin puree
- 946ml vegetable broth
- 120ml coconut milk
- Salt and pepper to taste
- Pumpkin seeds, toasted (for garnish)

Directions:
1. Preheat the Ninja Foodi Air Fryer to 190°C using the Air Roast function.
2. In the inner pot of the Ninja Foodi Pressure Cooker, heat olive oil using the SAUTÉ function.
3. Add chopped onion and minced garlic. Sauté until softened.
4. Stir in ground cumin, ground cinnamon, ground nutmeg, and cayenne pepper. Cook for another minute.
5. Pour in pumpkin puree and vegetable broth. Bring to a simmer.
6. Close the lid and set the pressure release valve to SEAL. Pressure cook on HIGH for 10 minutes.
7. Once done, quick release the pressure and carefully open the lid.
8. Stir in coconut milk.
9. Use an immersion blender to puree the soup until smooth.
10. Season with salt and pepper to taste.
11. Serve hot, garnished with toasted pumpkin seeds.

Nutrition: Calories: 200kcal; Fat: 12g; Carb: 20g; Protein: 4g

46. Broccoli Cheddar Soup

Preparation Time: 15 minutes
Cooking Time: 30 minutes
Servings: 4
Ingredients:

- 30g butter
- 1 onion, chopped
- 2 cloves garlic, minced
- 2 heads broccoli, chopped
- 946ml vegetable broth
- 240g heavy cream
- 500g shredded cheddar cheese
- Salt and pepper to taste
- Croutons (for garnish)

Directions:

1. Preheat the Ninja Foodi Air Fryer to 190°C using the Air Roast function.
2. In the inner pot of the Ninja Foodi Pressure Cooker, heat butter using the SAUTÉ function.
3. Add chopped onion and minced garlic. Sauté until softened.
4. Stir in chopped broccoli and vegetable broth. Bring to a simmer.
5. Close the lid and set the pressure release valve to SEAL. Pressure cook on HIGH for 5 minutes.
6. Once done, quick release the pressure and carefully open the lid.
7. Stir in heavy cream and shredded cheddar cheese.
8. Close the lid and let the soup sit for a few minutes to allow the cheese to melt.
9. Season with salt and pepper to taste.
10. Serve hot, garnished with croutons.

Nutrition: Calories: 380kcal; Fat: 30g; Carb: 15g; Protein: 12g

47. Cajun Shrimp Skewers

Preparation Time: 15 minutes

Cooking Time: 10 minutes

Servings: 4

Ingredients:

- 453g large shrimp, peeled and deveined
- 30ml olive oil
- 15g Cajun seasoning
- 1 lemon, sliced
- Salt and pepper to taste
- Wooden skewers, soaked in water

Directions:
1. Preheat the Ninja Foodi Air Fryer to 200°C using the Air Roast function.
2. In a bowl, toss the shrimp with olive oil and Cajun seasoning until evenly coated.
3. Thread the shrimp onto the soaked wooden skewers, alternating with slices of lemon.
4. Place the shrimp skewers in the Air Fryer basket in a single layer.
5. Air roast for 8-10 minutes until the shrimp are cooked through and slightly charred.
6. Season with salt and pepper to taste.
7. Serve hot as an appetizer or with your favorite side dishes.

Nutrition: Calories: 180kcal; Fat: 7g; Carb: 3g; Protein: 25g

48. Crispy Garlic Parmesan Chicken Wings

Preparation Time: 15 minutes

Cooking Time: 25 minutes

Servings: 4

Ingredients:

- 906g chicken wings
- 60g grated Parmesan cheese
- 30ml olive oil
- 4 cloves garlic, minced
- 7g dried oregano
- 7g dried thyme
- Salt and pepper to taste
- Fresh parsley, chopped (for garnish)

Directions:

1. Preheat the Ninja Foodi Air Fryer to 200°C using the Air Roast function.
2. In a bowl, toss the chicken wings with grated Parmesan cheese, olive oil, minced garlic, dried oregano, and dried thyme until evenly coated.
3. Place the chicken wings in the Air Fryer basket in a single layer, making sure they are not overcrowded.
4. Air roast for 20-25 minutes, flipping halfway through, until the wings are crispy and golden brown.
5. Season with salt and pepper to taste.
6. Serve hot, garnished with chopped fresh parsley.

Nutrition: Calories: 280kcal; Fat: 18g; Carb: 2g; Protein: 25g

49. Zucchini Fries

Preparation Time: 15 minutes

Cooking Time: 15 minutes

Servings: 4

Ingredients:

- 2 zucchinis, cut into sticks
- 120g breadcrumbs
- 60g grated Parmesan cheese
- 7g Italian seasoning
- 3.5g garlic powder
- 1.42g paprika
- Salt and pepper to taste
- 1 egg, beaten
- Cooking spray

Directions:

1. Preheat the Ninja Foodi Air Fryer to 200°C using the Air Roast function.
2. In a shallow dish, combine breadcrumbs, grated Parmesan cheese, Italian seasoning, garlic powder, paprika, salt, and pepper.

3. Dip each zucchini stick into the beaten egg, then coat with the breadcrumb mixture.
4. Place the coated zucchini sticks in the Air Fryer basket in a single layer.
5. Lightly spray the zucchini fries with cooking spray.
6. Air roast for 12-15 minutes until the zucchini fries are golden brown and crispy.
7. Serve hot, accompanied by your favorite dipping sauce.

Nutrition: Calories: 120kcal; Fat: 5g; Carb: 15g; Protein: 5g

50. Buffalo Cauliflower Bites

Preparation Time: 15 minutes
Cooking Time: 20 minutes
Servings: 4
Ingredients:

- 1 head cauliflower, cut into florets
- 120g all-purpose flour
- 120ml milk (or plant-based milk)
- 60ml hot sauce
- 30ml melted butter
- 7g garlic powder
- Salt and pepper to taste
- Ranch or blue cheese dressing (for serving)

Directions:
1. Preheat the Ninja Foodi Air Fryer to 200°C using the Air Roast function.
2. In a bowl, whisk together all-purpose flour, milk, hot sauce, melted butter, garlic powder, salt, and pepper until smooth.
3. Dip each cauliflower floret into the batter, making sure it is evenly coated.
4. Place the coated cauliflower florets in the Air Fryer basket in a single layer.
5. Air roast for 15-20 minutes until the cauliflower is tender and golden brown, flipping halfway through.
6. Serve hot, accompanied by ranch or blue cheese dressing for dipping.

Nutrition: Calories: 150kcal; Fat: 7g; Carb: 18g; Protein: 5g

51. Sweet Potato Fries

Preparation Time: 15 minutes
Cooking Time: 20 minutes
Servings: 4
Ingredients:

- 2 large sweet potatoes, cut into fries
- 30ml olive oil

- 7g smoked paprika
- 3.5g garlic powder
- 3.5g onion powder
- 1.42g cayenne pepper (optional)
- Salt and pepper to taste

Directions:
1. Preheat the Ninja Foodi Air Fryer to 200°C using the Air Roast function.
2. In a bowl, toss the sweet potato fries with olive oil, smoked paprika, garlic powder, onion powder, cayenne pepper (if using), salt, and pepper until evenly coated.
3. Place the seasoned sweet potato fries in the Air Fryer basket in a single layer.
4. Air roast for 18-20 minutes until the sweet potato fries are crispy and golden brown, shaking the basket halfway through.
5. Serve hot, accompanied by your favorite dipping sauce.

Nutrition: Calories: 160kcal; Fat: 7g; Carb: 23g; Protein: 2g

52. Avocado Fries

Preparation Time: 15 minutes
Cooking Time: 10 minutes
Servings: 4
Ingredients:

- 2 ripe avocados, sliced into wedges
- 120g all-purpose flour
- 2 eggs, beaten
- 240g breadcrumbs
- 7g garlic powder
- 3.5g paprika
- Salt and pepper to taste
- Cooking spray

Directions:
1. Preheat the Ninja Foodi Air Fryer to 200°C using the Air Roast function.
2. Set up a breading station with three shallow dishes: one with all-purpose flour.
3. Set up a breading station with three shallow dishes: one with all-purpose flour, one with beaten eggs, and one with breadcrumbs mixed with garlic powder, paprika, salt, and pepper.
4. Dredge each avocado wedge in flour, then dip it into the beaten eggs, and finally coat it with the breadcrumb mixture.
5. Place the breaded avocado wedges in the Air Fryer basket in a single layer.
6. Lightly spray the avocado fries with cooking spray.

7. Air fry for 8-10 minutes until the avocado fries are golden and crispy.
8. Serve hot, accompanied by your favorite dipping sauce.

Nutrition: Calories: 220kcal; Fat: 15g; Carb: 18g; Protein: 5g

53. Garlic Herb Potato Wedges

Preparation Time: 15 minutes
Cooking Time: 25 minutes
Servings: 4
Ingredients:

- 4 large potatoes, cut into wedges
- 30ml olive oil
- 2 cloves garlic, minced
- 7g dried rosemary
- 7g dried thyme
- 7g dried parsley
- Salt and pepper to taste

Directions:
1. Preheat the Ninja Foodi Air Fryer to 200°C using the Air Roast function.
2. In a large bowl, toss the potato wedges with olive oil, minced garlic, dried rosemary, dried thyme, dried parsley, salt, and pepper until evenly coated.
3. Place the seasoned potato wedges in the Air Fryer basket in a single layer.
4. Air roast for 20-25 minutes until the potato wedges are crispy and golden brown, flipping halfway through.
5. Serve hot, sprinkled with additional salt and pepper if desired.

Nutrition: Calories: 220kcal; Fat: 7g; Carb: 38g; Protein: 5g

54. Onion Rings

Preparation Time: 15 minutes
Cooking Time: 10 minutes
Servings: 4
Ingredients:

- 2 large onions, cut into rings
- 240g all-purpose flour
- 7g garlic powder
- 7g paprika
- 3.5g cayenne pepper
- 2 eggs, beaten

- 240g breadcrumbs
- Salt and pepper to taste
- Cooking spray

Directions:
1. Preheat the Ninja Foodi Air Fryer to 200°C using the Air Roast function.
2. In a shallow dish, combine all-purpose flour with garlic powder, paprika, cayenne pepper, salt, and pepper.
3. Set up a breading station with three shallow dishes: one with the seasoned flour, one with beaten eggs, and one with breadcrumbs.
4. Dredge each onion ring in the seasoned flour, then dip it into the beaten eggs, and finally coat it with breadcrumbs.
5. Place the breaded onion rings in the Air Fryer basket in a single layer.
6. Lightly spray the onion rings with cooking spray.
7. Air fry for 8-10 minutes until the onion rings are crispy and golden brown.
8. Serve hot, accompanied by your favorite dipping sauce.

Nutrition: Calories: 180kcal; Fat: 5g; Carb: 30g; Protein: 5g

55. Mozzarella Sticks

Preparation Time: 20 minutes
Cooking Time: 8 minutes
Servings: 4

Ingredients:

- 8 mozzarella cheese sticks
- 120g all-purpose flour
- 2 eggs, beaten
- 240g breadcrumbs
- 7g Italian seasoning
- 3.5g garlic powder
- Marinara sauce (for serving)

Directions:
1. Preheat the Ninja Foodi Air Fryer to 200°C using the Air Roast function.
2. Set up a breading station with three shallow dishes: one with all-purpose flour, one with beaten eggs, and one with breadcrumbs mixed with Italian seasoning and garlic powder.
3. Dredge each mozzarella stick in the flour, then dip it into the beaten eggs, and finally coat it with breadcrumbs.
4. Repeat the process for a thicker coating, if desired.
5. Place the breaded mozzarella sticks in the Air Fryer basket in a single layer.

6. Air fry for 6-8 minutes until the mozzarella sticks are golden and crispy.
7. Serve hot, accompanied by marinara sauce for dipping.

Nutrition: Calories: 250kcal; Fat: 12g; Carb: 20g; Protein: 12g

56. Jalapeno Poppers

Preparation Time: 20 minutes
Cooking Time: 10 minutes
Servings: 4
Ingredients:

- 8 jalapeno peppers
- 4 oz cream cheese, softened
- 120g shredded cheddar cheese
- 8 slices bacon, halved
- Toothpicks

Directions:
1. Preheat the Ninja Foodi Air Fryer to 190°C using the Air Roast function.
2. Cut jalapeno peppers in half lengthwise and remove the seeds and membranes.
3. In a bowl, mix together cream cheese and shredded cheddar cheese until well combined.
4. Stuff each jalapeno half with the cheese mixture.
5. Wrap each stuffed jalapeno half with a half slice of bacon and secure with a toothpick.
6. Place the stuffed jalapeno poppers in the Air Fryer basket in a single layer.
7. Air roast for 8-10 minutes until the bacon is crispy and the peppers are tender.
8. Serve hot as a delicious appetizer.

Nutrition: Calories: 180kcal; Fat: 15g; Carb: 4g; Protein: 8g

Chapter 5. Main Courses

57. Teriyaki Salmon Fillets

Preparation Time: 10 minutes

Cooking Time: 12 minutes

Servings: 4

Ingredients:

- 4 salmon fillets
- 60ml teriyaki sauce
- 30ml honey
- 15ml soy sauce
- 7g minced ginger
- 7g minced garlic
- Sesame seeds (for garnish)
- Sliced green onions (for garnish)

Directions:
1. Preheat the Ninja Foodi Air Fryer to 200°C using the Air Fry function.
2. In a bowl, mix together teriyaki sauce, honey, soy sauce, minced ginger, and minced garlic.
3. Place the salmon fillets in a shallow dish and pour the teriyaki marinade over them. Let them marinate for 10 minutes.
4. Place the marinated salmon fillets in the Air Fryer basket in a single layer.
5. Air fry for 10-12 minutes until the salmon is cooked through and flakes easily with a fork.
6. Garnish with sesame seeds and sliced green onions before serving.

Nutrition: Calories: 150kcal; Fat: 3g; Carb: 27g; Protein: 5g

58. Mushroom Risotto

Preparation Time: 15 minutes

Cooking Time: 20 minutes

Servings: 4

Ingredients:

- 15ml olive oil
- 1 onion, finely chopped
- 2 cloves garlic, minced
- 240g Arborio rice

- 120ml white wine (optional)
- 3 cups chicken or vegetable broth
- 8 oz mushrooms, sliced
- 60g grated Parmesan cheese
- Salt and pepper to taste
- Chopped fresh parsley (for garnish)

Directions:
1. Preheat the Ninja Foodi Air Fryer to 200°C using the Air Fry function.
2. In the inner pot of the Ninja Foodi Pressure Cooker, heat olive oil using the SAUTÉ function.
3. Add chopped onion and minced garlic. Sauté until softened.
4. Stir in Arborio rice and cook for 1-2 minutes until lightly toasted.
5. If using, pour in white wine and cook until it has evaporated.
6. Add chicken or vegetable broth and sliced mushrooms to the pot. Stir well.
7. Close the lid and set the pressure release valve to SEAL. Pressure cook on HIGH for 5 minutes.
8. Once done, quick release the pressure and carefully open the lid.
9. Stir in grated Parmesan cheese and season with salt and pepper to taste.
10. Serve hot, garnished with chopped fresh parsley.

Nutrition: Calories: 250kcal; Fat: 3g; Carb: 27g; Protein: 5g

59. Beef Stir Fry with Vegetables

Preparation Time: 15 minutes
Cooking Time: 15 minutes
Servings: 4
Ingredients:

- 453g beef sirloin, thinly sliced
- 30ml soy sauce
- 15ml hoisin sauce
- 15ml oyster sauce
- 15g cornstarch
- 30ml vegetable oil
- 2 cloves garlic, minced
- 1 onion, sliced
- 1 bell pepper, sliced
- 240g broccoli florets
- Salt and pepper to taste
- Cooked rice (for serving)

Directions:

1. Preheat the Ninja Foodi Air Fryer to 200°C using the Air Fry function.
2. In a bowl, mix together soy sauce, hoisin sauce, oyster sauce, and cornstarch.
3. Add thinly sliced beef sirloin to the bowl and toss to coat with the marinade. Let it marinate for 10 minutes.
4. Place marinated beef slices in the Air Fryer basket in a single layer.
5. Air fry for 8-10 minutes until the beef is browned and cooked through. Remove and set aside.
6. In the same Air Fryer basket, add vegetable oil, minced garlic, sliced onion, sliced bell pepper, and broccoli florets.
7. Air fry for 5-7 minutes until the vegetables are tender.

Nutrition: Calories: 320kcal; Fat: 13g; Carb: 27g; Protein: 5g

60. Shrimp Scampi

Preparation Time: 10 minutes
Cooking Time: 10 minutes
Servings: 4
Ingredients:

- 453g large shrimp, peeled and deveined
- 60g unsalted butter
- 4 cloves garlic, minced
- 60ml white wine (optional)
- 30ml lemon juice
- 30g chopped fresh parsley
- Salt and pepper to taste
- Cooked pasta or crusty bread (for serving)

Directions:
1. Preheat the Ninja Foodi Air Fryer to 200°C using the Air Fry function.
2. In a bowl, toss the shrimp with salt, pepper, and half of the minced garlic.
3. Place the shrimp in the Air Fryer basket in a single layer.
4. Air fry for 5-7 minutes until the shrimp are pink and cooked through.
5. In a skillet, melt the butter over medium heat. Add the remaining minced garlic and cook until fragrant.
6. If using, pour in white wine and lemon juice. Bring to a simmer.
7. Add the cooked shrimp to the skillet and toss to coat in the sauce.
8. Sprinkle chopped fresh parsley over the shrimp.
9. Serve hot, over cooked pasta or with crusty bread.

Nutrition: Calories: 230kcal; Fat: 12g; Carb: 4g; Protein: 25g

61. Vegetable Lasagna

Preparation Time: 20 minutes

Cooking Time: 25 minutes

Servings: 6

Ingredients:

- 9 lasagna noodles, cooked according to package instructions
- 500ml marinara sauce
- 500g ricotta cheese
- 240g shredded mozzarella cheese
- 240g chopped mixed vegetables (such as spinach, zucchini, bell peppers)
- 60g grated Parmesan cheese
- 7g dried basil
- 7g dried oregano
- Salt and pepper to taste

Directions:

1. Preheat the Ninja Foodi Air Fryer to 190°C using the Air Roast function.
2. In a bowl, mix together ricotta cheese, shredded mozzarella cheese, chopped mixed vegetables, grated Parmesan cheese, dried basil, dried oregano, salt, and pepper.
3. Spread a thin layer of marinara sauce on the bottom of the Air Fryer basket.
4. Place 3 cooked lasagna noodles on top of the marinara sauce.
5. Spread half of the ricotta mixture over the noodles.
6. Repeat the layers with marinara sauce, noodles, and remaining ricotta mixture.
7. Finish with a final layer of marinara sauce and sprinkle with additional shredded mozzarella cheese.
8. Cover the Air Fryer basket with aluminum foil.
9. Air roast for 20-25 minutes until the lasagna is heated through and the cheese is melted and bubbly.
10. Let it rest for a few minutes before slicing and serving.

Nutrition: Calories: 340kcal; Fat: 15g; Carb: 30g; Protein: 18g

62. Honey Garlic Glazed Ham

Preparation Time: 10 minutes

Cooking Time: 30 minutes

Servings: 6

Ingredients:

- 1 pre-cooked ham (about 3-4 lbs)
- 60ml honey
- 30ml soy sauce

- 30g Dijon mustard
- 2 cloves garlic, minced
- 15ml apple cider vinegar
- 7g dried thyme
- 3.5g ground ginger
- 1.42g black pepper
- Pineapple rings (for garnish)
- Maraschino cherries (for garnish)

Directions:
1. Preheat the Ninja Foodi Air Fryer to 190°C using the Air Roast function.
2. In a bowl, whisk together honey, soy sauce, Dijon mustard, minced garlic, apple cider vinegar, dried thyme, ground ginger, and black pepper.
3. Place the pre-cooked ham in the Air Fryer basket.
4. Brush the honey garlic glaze over the ham, making sure it is evenly coated.
5. Arrange pineapple rings and maraschino cherries on top of the ham, securing them with toothpicks if needed.
6. Air roast for 25-30 minutes until the ham is heated through and the glaze is caramelized.
7. Let it rest for a few minutes before slicing and serving.

Nutrition: Calories: 280kcal; Fat: 15g; Carb: 15g; Protein: 25g

63. Lemon Butter Cod

Preparation Time: 10 minutes
Cooking Time: 12 minutes
Servings: 4
Ingredients:

- 4 cod fillets
- 60g unsalted butter, melted
- 30ml lemon juice
- 2 cloves garlic, minced
- 7g lemon zest
- 7g dried parsley
- Salt and pepper to taste
- Lemon slices (for garnish)
- Fresh parsley, chopped (for garnish)

Directions:
1. Preheat the Ninja Foodi Air Fryer to 190°C using the Air Fry function.

2. In a bowl, whisk together melted butter, lemon juice, minced garlic, lemon zest, dried parsley, salt, and pepper.
3. Place the cod fillets in the Air Fryer basket in a single layer.
4. Pour the lemon butter mixture over the cod fillets, making sure they are evenly coated.
5. Air fry for 10-12 minutes until the cod is cooked through and flakes easily with a fork.
6. Garnish with lemon slices and chopped fresh parsley before serving.

Nutrition: Calories: 220kcal; Fat: 12g; Carb: 3g; Protein: 25g

64. Beef and Broccoli

Preparation Time: 15 minutes

Cooking Time: 15 minutes

Servings: 4

Ingredients:

- 453g beef sirloin, thinly sliced
- 3 cups broccoli florets
- 30ml soy sauce
- 15ml oyster sauce
- 15ml hoisin sauce
- 15g cornstarch
- 2 cloves garlic, minced
- 7g minced ginger
- 30ml vegetable oil
- Sesame seeds (for garnish)
- Sliced green onions (for garnish)
- Cooked rice (for serving)

Directions:

1. Preheat the Ninja Foodi Air Fryer to 200°C using the Air Fry function.
2. In a bowl, mix together soy sauce, oyster sauce, hoisin sauce, cornstarch, minced garlic, and minced ginger.
3. Add thinly sliced beef sirloin to the bowl and toss to coat with the marinade. Let it marinate for 10 minutes.
4. Place the marinated beef slices in the Air Fryer basket in a single layer.
5. Air fry for 8-10 minutes until the beef is browned and cooked through. Remove and set aside.
6. In the same Air Fryer basket, add broccoli florets and drizzle with vegetable oil. Toss to coat.
7. Air fry for 5-7 minutes until the broccoli is tender-crisp.
8. Return the cooked beef to the Air Fryer basket with the broccoli.
9. Stir well to combine and garnish with sesame seeds and sliced green onions.

10. Serve hot, over cooked rice.

Nutrition: Calories: 320kcal; Fat: 16g; Carb: 15g; Protein: 28g

65. Chicken Fajitas

Preparation Time: 15 minutes

Cooking Time: 15 minutes

Servings: 4

Ingredients:

- 453g chicken breast, thinly sliced
- 1 bell pepper, sliced
- 1 onion, sliced
- 30ml olive oil
- 15g chili powder
- 7g ground cumin
- 7g smoked paprika
- 7g garlic powder
- 3.5g onion powder
- Salt and pepper to taste
- Flour tortillas (for serving)
- Salsa, guacamole, sour cream (for serving)

Directions:

1. Preheat the Ninja Foodi Air Fryer to 200°C using the Air Fry function.
2. In a bowl, toss together thinly sliced chicken breast, sliced bell pepper, sliced onion, olive oil, chili powder, ground cumin, smoked paprika, garlic powder, onion powder, salt, and pepper until evenly coated.
3. Place the seasoned chicken and vegetables in the Air Fryer basket in a single layer.
4. Air fry for 12-15 minutes until the chicken is cooked through and the vegetables are tender.
5. Warm the flour tortillas in the Air Fryer for 1-2 minutes, if desired.
6. Serve the chicken and vegetables in warm tortillas, accompanied by salsa, guacamole, and sour cream.

Nutrition: Calories: 240kcal; Fat: 10g; Carb: 10g; Protein: 25g

66. Spinach and Ricotta Stuffed Chicken Breast

Preparation Time: 20 minutes

Cooking Time: 20 minutes

Servings: 4

Ingredients:

- 4 boneless, skinless chicken breasts

- 240g ricotta cheese
- 240g chopped spinach
- 60g grated Parmesan cheese
- 7g minced garlic
- 3.5g dried basil
- 3.5g dried oregano
- Salt and pepper to taste
- 240ml marinara sauce
- 240g shredded mozzarella cheese

Directions:
1. Preheat the Ninja Foodi Air Fryer to 190°C using the Air Fry function.
2. In a bowl, combine ricotta cheese, chopped spinach, grated Parmesan cheese, minced garlic, dried basil, dried oregano, salt, and pepper.
3. Slice a pocket into each chicken breast and stuff with the spinach and ricotta mixture.
4. Place the stuffed chicken breasts in the Air Fryer basket in a single layer.
5. Air fry for 15-18 minutes until the chicken is cooked through.
6. Top each chicken breast with marinara sauce and shredded mozzarella cheese.
7. Air fry for an additional 3-5 minutes until the cheese is melted and bubbly.
8. Serve hot, accompanied by your favorite side dishes.

Nutrition: Calories: 320kcal; Fat: 14g; Carb: 8g; Protein: 40g

67. Coconut Curry Chicken

Preparation Time: 15 minutes
Cooking Time: 25 minutes
Servings: 4
Ingredients:

- 453g chicken breasts, cubed
- 1 onion, chopped
- 2 cloves garlic, minced
- 1 bell pepper, sliced
- 1 zucchini, sliced
- 240ml coconut milk
- 30g red curry paste
- 15ml fish sauce
- 15g brown sugar
- 15ml lime juice
- 15ml vegetable oil

- Cooked rice (for serving)
- Chopped fresh cilantro (for garnish)

Directions:
1. Preheat the Ninja Foodi Air Fryer to 190°C using the Air Fry function.
2. In a bowl, mix together coconut milk, red curry paste, fish sauce, brown sugar, and lime juice to make the curry sauce.
3. Heat vegetable oil in the Air Fryer basket. Add chopped onion and minced garlic. Cook until softened.
4. Add cubed chicken breasts to the Air Fryer basket and cook until browned.
5. Add sliced bell pepper and zucchini to the Air Fryer basket.
6. Pour the curry sauce over the chicken and vegetables in the Air Fryer basket.
7. Air fry for 20-25 minutes until the chicken is cooked through and the vegetables are tender.
8. Serve hot, over cooked rice, and garnish with chopped fresh cilantro.

Nutrition: Calories: 280kcal; Fat: 18g; Carb: 10g; Protein: 25g

68. Beef Stroganoff

Preparation Time: 15 minutes
Cooking Time: 20 minutes
Servings: 4
Ingredients:

- 453g beef sirloin, thinly sliced
- 8 oz mushrooms, sliced
- 1 onion, thinly sliced
- 2 cloves garlic, minced
- 240ml beef broth
- 240g sour cream
- 30g all-purpose flour
- 30ml Worcestershire sauce
- 7g Dijon mustard
- Salt and pepper to taste
- Cooked egg noodles or rice (for serving)
- Chopped fresh parsley (for garnish)

Directions:
1. Preheat the Ninja Foodi Air Fryer to 190°C using the Air Fry function.
2. Place thinly sliced beef sirloin in the Air Fryer basket in a single layer.
3. Air fry for 8-10 minutes until the beef is browned and cooked through. Remove and set aside.
4. In the same Air Fryer basket, add sliced mushrooms, thinly sliced onion, and minced garlic.
5. Air fry for 5-7 minutes until the vegetables are tender.

6. In a bowl, whisk together beef broth, sour cream, all-purpose flour, Worcestershire sauce, Dijon mustard, salt, and pepper.
7. Pour the sour cream mixture over the cooked beef and vegetables in the Air Fryer basket.
8. Air fry for an additional 3-5 minutes until the sauce thickens.
9. Serve hot, over cooked egg noodles or rice, and garnish with chopped fresh parsley.

Nutrition: Calories: 380kcal; Fat: 20g; Carb: 15g; Protein: 30g

69. Jambalaya

Preparation Time: 15 minutes
Cooking Time: 25 minutes
Servings: 6
Ingredients:

- 453g shrimp, peeled and deveined
- 453g chicken sausage, sliced
- 1 onion, chopped
- 1 bell pepper, chopped
- 2 celery stalks, chopped
- 2 cloves garlic, minced
- 240g long-grain rice
- 1 can (14 oz) diced tomatoes
- 240ml chicken broth
- 15g Cajun seasoning
- 7g dried thyme
- 1 bay leaf
- Salt and pepper to taste
- Chopped fresh parsley (for garnish)

Directions:
1. Preheat the Ninja Foodi Air Fryer to 190°C using the Air Fry function.
2. In the Air Fryer basket, combine shrimp, chicken sausage, chopped onion, chopped bell pepper, chopped celery, minced garlic, long-grain rice, diced tomatoes, chicken broth, Cajun seasoning, dried thyme, bay leaf, salt, and pepper.
3. Stir well to combine all ingredients.
4. Air fry for 20-25 minutes until the rice is cooked and the shrimp is pink and cooked through.
5. Remove the bay leaf before serving.
6. Garnish with chopped fresh parsley before serving.

Nutrition: Calories: 320kcal; Fat: 10g; Carb: 30g; Protein: 25g

70. Mediterranean Quinoa Salad

Preparation Time: 15 minutes

Cooking Time: 15 minutes (for quinoa)

Servings: 4

Ingredients:

- 240g quinoa
- 500ml water or vegetable broth
- 1 cucumber, diced
- 1 bell pepper, diced
- 240g cherry tomatoes, halved
- 120g Kalamata olives, sliced
- 60g red onion, thinly sliced
- 60g feta cheese, crumbled
- 30g chopped fresh parsley
- 30ml extra virgin olive oil
- 15ml lemon juice
- 7g dried oregano
- Salt and pepper to taste

Directions:

1. Rinse quinoa under cold water. In a pot, combine quinoa and water or vegetable broth.
2. Bring to a boil, then reduce heat to low, cover, and simmer for 15 minutes until quinoa is cooked and water is absorbed. Fluff with a fork and let it cool.
3. In a large bowl, combine cooked quinoa, diced cucumber, diced bell pepper, halved cherry tomatoes, sliced Kalamata olives, thinly sliced red onion, crumbled feta cheese, and chopped fresh parsley.
4. In a small bowl, whisk together extra virgin olive oil, lemon juice, dried oregano, salt, and pepper.
5. Pour the dressing over the salad and toss to coat evenly.
6. Serve chilled or at room temperature.

Nutrition: Calories: 320kcal; Fat: 15g; Carb: 40g; Protein: 8g

71. Sausage and Peppers

Preparation Time: 10 minutes

Cooking Time: 20 minutes

Servings: 4

Ingredients:

- 453g Italian sausage links
- 2 bell peppers, sliced

- 1 onion, sliced
- 30ml olive oil
- 7g Italian seasoning
- Salt and pepper to taste
- Hoagie rolls (for serving)

Directions:
1. Preheat the Ninja Foodi Air Fryer to 190°C using the Air Fry function.
2. Place Italian sausage links in the Air Fryer basket.
3. Air fry for 15-20 minutes until the sausages are browned and cooked through.
4. In a bowl, toss sliced bell peppers and onions with olive oil, Italian seasoning, salt, and pepper.
5. Add the seasoned bell peppers and onions to the Air Fryer basket with the sausages.
6. Air fry for an additional 5-7 minutes until the vegetables are tender.
7. Serve the sausage and peppers in hoagie rolls.

Nutrition: Calories: 320kcal; Fat: 25g; Carb: 10g; Protein: 15g

72. Teriyaki Chicken and Vegetables

Preparation Time: 15 minutes
Cooking Time: 20 minutes
Servings: 4
Ingredients:

- 453g chicken breast, cubed
- 500g mixed vegetables (such as bell peppers, broccoli, carrots)
- 60ml teriyaki sauce
- 30ml soy sauce
- 30ml honey
- 15g sesame oil
- 15g cornstarch
- 7g minced ginger
- 7g minced garlic
- Cooked rice (for serving)
- Sesame seeds (for garnish)
- Sliced green onions (for garnish)

Directions:
1. Preheat the Ninja Foodi Air Fryer to 190°C using the Air Fry function.
2. In a bowl, whisk together teriyaki sauce, soy sauce, honey, sesame oil, cornstarch, minced ginger, and minced garlic.
3. Add cubed chicken breast and mixed vegetables to the bowl. Toss to coat evenly.

4. Place the chicken and vegetable mixture in the Air Fryer basket.
5. Air fry for 15-20 minutes until the chicken is cooked through and the vegetables are tender.
6. Serve hot, over cooked rice, and garnish with sesame seeds and sliced green onions.

Nutrition: Calories: 280kcal; Fat: 10g; Carb: 20g; Protein: 25g

73. Lemon Garlic Shrimp Pasta

Preparation Time: 15 minutes
Cooking Time: 15 minutes
Servings: 4
Ingredients:

- 8 oz spaghetti or linguine pasta
- 453g shrimp, peeled and deveined
- 60g unsalted butter
- 4 cloves garlic, minced
- Zest of 1 lemon
- Juice of 1 lemon
- 60g chopped fresh parsley
- Salt and pepper to taste
- Grated Parmesan cheese (for serving)

Directions:

1. Cook pasta according to package instructions. Drain and set aside.
2. Preheat the Ninja Foodi Air Fryer to 190°C using the Air Fry function.
3. In the Air Fryer basket, combine peeled and deveined shrimp, minced garlic, lemon zest, lemon juice, chopped fresh parsley, salt, and pepper.
4. Air fry for 5-7 minutes until the shrimp is pink and cooked through.
5. In a skillet, melt unsalted butter over medium heat. Add cooked pasta and cooked shrimp mixture to the skillet. Toss to coat evenly.
6. Serve hot, sprinkled with grated Parmesan cheese.

Nutrition: Calories: 380kcal; Fat: 15g; Carb: 40g; Protein: 25g

Chapter 6. One-Pot Meals

74. Creamy Tuscan Chicken

Preparation Time: 15 minutes

Cooking Time: 20 minutes

Servings: 4

Ingredients:

- 453g chicken breasts, thinly sliced
- 15ml olive oil
- 2 cloves garlic, minced
- 240g sun-dried tomatoes, drained and sliced
- 240g spinach leaves
- 240g heavy cream
- 120g grated Parmesan cheese
- Salt and pepper to taste
- Cooked pasta (for serving)
- Chopped fresh basil (for garnish)

Directions:

1. Preheat the Ninja Foodi Air Fryer to 190°C using the Air Fry function.
2. Heat olive oil in the Air Fryer basket. Add minced garlic and cook until fragrant.
3. Add thinly sliced chicken breasts to the Air Fryer basket. Cook until browned and cooked through.
4. Stir in sun-dried tomatoes and spinach leaves.
5. Pour heavy cream over the chicken mixture in the Air Fryer basket.
6. Sprinkle grated Parmesan cheese over the top.
7. Air fry for an additional 5-7 minutes until the sauce is heated through and slightly thickened.
8. Serve hot, over cooked pasta, and garnish with chopped fresh basil.

Nutrition: Calories: 350kcal; Fat: 20g; Carb: 10g; Protein: 30g

75. Spicy Sausage and Rice Skillet

Preparation Time: 10 minutes

Cooking Time: 25 minutes

Servings: 4

Ingredients:

- 453g spicy sausage links, sliced

- 1 onion, chopped
- 1 bell pepper, chopped
- 2 cloves garlic, minced
- 240g long-grain rice
- 500ml chicken broth
- 1 can (14 oz) diced tomatoes
- 7g Cajun seasoning
- Salt and pepper to taste
- Chopped fresh parsley (for garnish)

Directions:
1. Preheat the Ninja Foodi Air Fryer to 190°C using the Air Fry function.
2. Place sliced spicy sausage links in the Air Fryer basket. Air fry for 10-12 minutes until browned.
3. In the same Air Fryer basket, add chopped onion, chopped bell pepper, and minced garlic. Cook until softened.
4. Stir in long-grain rice and cook for 2-3 minutes until lightly toasted.
5. Pour in chicken broth, diced tomatoes (with juices), Cajun seasoning, salt, and pepper.
6. Stir to combine all ingredients.
7. Air fry for 15-20 minutes until the rice is cooked and the liquid is absorbed.
8. Serve hot, garnished with chopped fresh parsley.

Nutrition: Calories: 380kcal; Fat: 22g; Carb: 30g; Protein: 18g

76. BBQ Chicken and Potatoes

Preparation Time: 10 minutes
Cooking Time: 30 minutes
Servings: 4
Ingredients:

- 4 boneless, skinless chicken breasts
- 4 medium potatoes, cubed
- 240ml BBQ sauce
- 30ml olive oil
- 7g smoked paprika
- 7g garlic powder
- Salt and pepper to taste
- Chopped fresh parsley (for garnish)

Directions:
1. Preheat the Ninja Foodi Air Fryer to 190°C using the Air Fry function.
2. In a bowl, toss cubed potatoes with olive oil, smoked paprika, garlic powder, salt, and pepper.

3. Place seasoned potatoes in the Air Fryer basket. Air fry for 15 minutes, shaking halfway through.
4. Season chicken breasts with salt and pepper.
5. Remove the Air Fryer basket and add chicken breasts to the basket. Brush BBQ sauce over the chicken.
6. Return the basket to the Air Fryer. Air fry for an additional 15 minutes or until chicken is cooked through.
7. Serve hot, garnished with chopped fresh parsley.

Nutrition: Calories: 380kcal; Fat: 10g; Carb: 40g; Protein: 30g

77. Lemon Garlic Shrimp Scampi

Preparation Time: 10 minutes
Cooking Time: 15 minutes
Servings: 4
Ingredients:

- 453g shrimp, peeled and deveined
- 8 oz linguine pasta
- 60g unsalted butter
- 4 cloves garlic, minced
- Zest of 1 lemon
- Juice of 1 lemon
- 60g chopped fresh parsley
- Salt and pepper to taste
- Grated Parmesan cheese (for serving)

Directions:
1. Preheat the Ninja Foodi Air Fryer to 190°C using the Air Fry function.
2. Cook linguine pasta according to package instructions. Drain and set aside.
3. In the Air Fryer basket, combine peeled and deveined shrimp, minced garlic, lemon zest, lemon juice, chopped fresh parsley, salt, and pepper.
4. Air fry for 5-7 minutes until the shrimp is pink and cooked through.
5. In a skillet, melt unsalted butter over medium heat. Add cooked pasta and cooked shrimp mixture to the skillet. Toss to coat evenly.
6. Serve hot, sprinkled with grated Parmesan cheese.

Nutrition: Calories: 320kcal; Fat: 15g; Carb: 30g; Protein: 25g

78. Beef and Vegetable Stir Fry

Preparation Time: 15 minutes
Cooking Time: 20 minutes
Servings: 4

Ingredients:

- 453g beef sirloin, thinly sliced
- 500g mixed vegetables (such as bell peppers, broccoli, snap peas)
- 60ml soy sauce
- 30ml hoisin sauce
- 30ml oyster sauce
- 15g cornstarch
- 2 cloves garlic, minced
- 7g minced ginger
- 30ml vegetable oil
- Cooked rice (for serving)

Directions:

1. Preheat the Ninja Foodi Air Fryer to 190°C using the Air Fry function.
2. In a bowl, mix together soy sauce, hoisin sauce, oyster sauce, cornstarch, minced garlic, and minced ginger.
3. Add thinly sliced beef sirloin to the bowl and toss to coat with the marinade. Let it marinate for 10 minutes.
4. Heat vegetable oil in a skillet over medium-high heat. Add marinated beef slices and cook until browned.
5. Add mixed vegetables to the skillet and stir-fry until tender-crisp.
6. Pour any remaining marinade into the skillet and stir until thickened.
7. Serve hot, over cooked rice.

Nutrition: Calories: 350kcal; Fat: 15g; Carb: 20g; Protein: 25g

79. Creamy Tuscan Chicken Pasta

Preparation Time: 15 minutes
Cooking Time: 20 minutes
Servings: 4
Ingredients:

- 453g chicken breasts, thinly sliced
- 8 oz penne pasta
- 240g sun-dried tomatoes, drained and sliced
- 240g spinach leaves
- 240g heavy cream
- 120g grated Parmesan cheese
- 30ml olive oil
- 2 cloves garlic, minced

- Salt and pepper to taste

Directions:
1. Preheat the Ninja Foodi Air Fryer to 190°C using the Air Fry function.
2. Cook penne pasta according to package instructions. Drain and set aside.
3. In the Air Fryer basket, combine thinly sliced chicken breasts, olive oil, minced garlic, salt, and pepper.
4. Air fry for 8-10 minutes until the chicken is cooked through.
5. Stir in sun-dried tomatoes and spinach leaves.
6. Pour heavy cream over the chicken mixture in the Air Fryer basket.
7. Sprinkle grated Parmesan cheese over the top.
8. Air fry for an additional 5-7 minutes until the sauce is heated through and slightly thickened.
9. Serve hot, over cooked penne pasta.

Nutrition: Calories: 380kcal; Fat: 20g; Carb: 10g; Protein: 30g

80. Veggie-Packed Fried Rice

Preparation Time: 15 minutes
Cooking Time: 15 minutes
Servings: 4

Ingredients:
- 500g cooked rice (preferably cold)
- 240g mixed vegetables (such as peas, carrots, corn)
- 2 eggs, beaten
- 30ml soy sauce
- 15ml sesame oil
- 15ml vegetable oil
- 2 cloves garlic, minced
- 7g minced ginger
- 2 green onions, chopped
- Salt and pepper to taste

Directions:
1. Preheat the Ninja Foodi Air Fryer to 190°C using the Air Fry function.
2. Heat vegetable oil in the Air Fryer basket. Add minced garlic and minced ginger. Cook until fragrant.
3. Add mixed vegetables to the Air Fryer basket and cook until tender.
4. Push the vegetables to one side of the Air Fryer basket. Pour beaten eggs into the empty side.
5. Scramble the eggs until cooked.
6. Add cooked rice to the Air Fryer basket, along with soy sauce, sesame oil, chopped green onions, salt, and pepper.
7. Toss everything together until well combined.

8. Air fry for 10-12 minutes, stirring occasionally, until the rice is heated through and slightly crispy.
9. Serve hot.

Nutrition: Calories: 250kcal; Fat: 8g; Carb: 35g; Protein: 8g

81. Italian Sausage and Tortellini Soup

Preparation Time: 10 minutes

Cooking Time: 20 minutes

Servings: 6

Ingredients:

- 453g Italian sausage, casings removed
- 1 onion, chopped
- 2 cloves garlic, minced
- 946ml chicken broth
- 1 can (14 oz) diced tomatoes
- 1 package (9 oz) cheese tortellini
- 500g chopped spinach
- 7g Italian seasoning
- Salt and pepper to taste
- Grated Parmesan cheese (for serving)

Directions:

1. Preheat the Ninja Foodi Air Fryer to 190°C using the Air Fry function.
2. Cook Italian sausage in the Air Fryer basket until browned and cooked through.
3. Add chopped onion and minced garlic to the Air Fryer basket. Cook until softened.
4. Pour in chicken broth, diced tomatoes (with juices), cheese tortellini, chopped spinach, Italian seasoning, salt, and pepper.
5. Stir to combine all ingredients.
6. Air fry for 15-20 minutes until the tortellini are cooked and the soup is heated through.
7. Serve hot, garnished with grated Parmesan cheese.

Nutrition: Calories: 280kcal; Fat: 12g; Carb: 25g; Protein: 15g

82. Chicken and Broccoli Rice Casserole

Preparation Time: 15 minutes

Cooking Time: 25 minutes

Servings: 4

Ingredients:

- 453g chicken breast, cubed
- 240g white rice, uncooked

- 500ml chicken broth
- 500g broccoli florets
- 240g shredded cheddar cheese
- 120g sour cream
- 60g mayonnaise
- 15ml olive oil
- 2 cloves garlic, minced
- Salt and pepper to taste

Directions:
1. Preheat the Ninja Foodi Air Fryer to 190°C using the Air Fry function.
2. In the Air Fryer basket, combine cubed chicken breast, olive oil, minced garlic, salt, and pepper.
3. Air fry for 10-12 minutes until the chicken is cooked through.
4. Remove the Air Fryer basket and set aside the cooked chicken.
5. In the same Air Fryer basket, add white rice and chicken broth.
6. Air fry for 10 minutes, stirring halfway through.
7. Add broccoli florets to the Air Fryer basket. Air fry for an additional 5 minutes until the rice is cooked and the broccoli is tender.
8. Stir in cooked chicken, shredded cheddar cheese, sour cream, and mayonnaise until well combined.
9. Air fry for another 5 minutes until the cheese is melted and bubbly.
10. Serve hot.

Nutrition: Calories: 380kcal; Fat: 20g; Carb: 25g; Protein: 30g

83. Lemon Garlic Butter Shrimp and Asparagus

Preparation Time: 10 minutes
Cooking Time: 15 minutes
Servings: 4
Ingredients:

- 453g shrimp, peeled and deveined
- 1 bunch asparagus, trimmed
- 60g unsalted butter, melted
- 4 cloves garlic, minced
- Zest of 1 lemon
- Juice of 1 lemon
- Salt and pepper to taste
- Chopped fresh parsley (for garnish)

Directions:
1. Preheat the Ninja Foodi Air Fryer to 190°C using the Air Fry function.

2. In a bowl, combine peeled and deveined shrimp, trimmed asparagus, melted butter, minced garlic, lemon zest, lemon juice, salt, and pepper.
3. Toss until well coated.
4. Spread the shrimp and asparagus mixture in a single layer in the Air Fryer basket.
5. Air fry for 10-12 minutes, shaking halfway through, until the shrimp is pink and cooked through, and the asparagus is tender.
6. Serve hot, garnished with chopped fresh parsley.

Nutrition: Calories: 280kcal; Fat: 15g; Carb: 10g; Protein: 25g

84. Creamy Mushroom Risotto

Preparation Time: 10 minutes
Cooking Time: 25 minutes
Servings: 4
Ingredients:

- 240g Arborio rice
- 500ml chicken or vegetable broth
- 8 oz mushrooms, sliced
- 1 onion, chopped
- 2 cloves garlic, minced
- 60g grated Parmesan cheese
- 30g unsalted butter
- 15ml olive oil
- 60ml dry white wine (optional)
- Salt and pepper to taste
- Chopped fresh parsley (for garnish)

Directions:

1. Preheat the Ninja Foodi Air Fryer to 190°C using the Air Fry function.
2. In the Air Fryer basket, combine sliced mushrooms, chopped onion, minced garlic, and olive oil.
3. Air fry for 10-12 minutes until the mushrooms are golden brown and the onions are softened.
4. Remove the Air Fryer basket and set aside half of the cooked mushrooms for garnish.
5. Add Arborio rice to the remaining mushrooms in the Air Fryer basket. Stir to coat the rice with the oil and juices from the mushrooms.
6. Pour in chicken or vegetable broth (and dry white wine if using). Stir to combine.
7. Air fry for 15-18 minutes, stirring occasionally, until the rice is cooked and creamy.
8. Stir in grated Parmesan cheese and unsalted butter until melted and creamy.
9. Season with salt and pepper to taste.
10. Serve hot, garnished with the reserved cooked mushrooms and chopped fresh parsley.

Nutrition: Calories: 320kcal; Fat: 15g; Carb: 35g; Protein: 8g

85. Beef and Vegetable Stir Fry

Preparation Time: 15 minutes
Cooking Time: 20 minutes
Servings: 4
Ingredients:

- 453g beef sirloin, thinly sliced
- 500g mixed vegetables (such as bell peppers, broccoli, snap peas)
- 60ml soy sauce
- 30ml hoisin sauce
- 30ml oyster sauce
- 15g cornstarch
- 2 cloves garlic, minced
- 7g minced ginger
- 30ml vegetable oil
- Cooked rice (for serving)

Directions:
1. Preheat the Ninja Foodi Air Fryer to 190°C using the Air Fry function.
2. In a bowl, mix together soy sauce, hoisin sauce, oyster sauce, cornstarch, minced garlic, and minced ginger.
3. Add thinly sliced beef sirloin to the bowl and toss to coat with the marinade. Let it marinate for 10 minutes.
4. Heat vegetable oil in a skillet over medium-high heat. Add marinated beef slices and cook until browned.
5. Add mixed vegetables to the skillet and stir-fry until tender-crisp.
6. Pour any remaining marinade into the skillet and stir until thickened.
7. Serve hot, over cooked rice.

Nutrition: Calories: 350kcal; Fat: 15g; Carb: 20g; Protein: 25g

86. Creamy Tuscan Chicken Pasta

Preparation Time: 15 minutes
Cooking Time: 20 minutes
Servings: 4
Ingredients:

- 453g chicken breasts, thinly sliced

- 8 oz penne pasta
- 240g sun-dried tomatoes, drained and sliced
- 240g spinach leaves
- 240g heavy cream
- 120g grated Parmesan cheese
- 30ml olive oil
- 2 cloves garlic, minced
- Salt and pepper to taste

Directions:
1. Preheat the Ninja Foodi Air Fryer to 190°C using the Air Fry function.
2. Cook penne pasta according to package instructions. Drain and set aside.
3. In the Air Fryer basket, combine thinly sliced chicken breasts, olive oil, minced garlic, salt, and pepper.
4. Air fry for 8-10 minutes until the chicken is cooked through.
5. Stir in sun-dried tomatoes and spinach leaves.
6. Pour heavy cream over the chicken mixture in the Air Fryer basket.
7. Sprinkle grated Parmesan cheese over the top.
8. Air fry for an additional 5-7 minutes until the sauce is heated through and slightly thickened.
9. Serve hot, over cooked penne pasta.

Nutrition: Calories: 380kcal; Fat: 20g; Carb: 10g; Protein: 30g

87. Veggie-Packed Fried Rice

Preparation Time: 15 minutes

Cooking Time: 15 minutes

Servings: 4

Ingredients:

- 500g cooked rice (preferably cold)
- 240g mixed vegetables (such as peas, carrots, corn)
- 2 eggs, beaten
- 30ml soy sauce
- 15ml sesame oil
- 15ml vegetable oil
- 2 cloves garlic, minced
- 7g minced ginger
- 2 green onions, chopped
- Salt and pepper to taste

Directions:
1. Preheat the Ninja Foodi Air Fryer to 190°C using the Air Fry function.

2. Heat vegetable oil in the Air Fryer basket. Add minced garlic and minced ginger. Cook until fragrant.
3. Add mixed vegetables to the Air Fryer basket and cook until tender.
4. Push the vegetables to one side of the Air Fryer basket. Pour beaten eggs into the empty side. Scramble the eggs until cooked.
5. Add cooked rice to the Air Fryer basket, along with soy sauce, sesame oil, chopped green onions, salt, and pepper.
6. Toss everything together until well combined.
7. Air fry for 10-12 minutes, stirring occasionally, until the rice is heated through and slightly crispy.
8. Serve hot.

Nutrition: Calories: 250kcal; Fat: 8g; Carb: 35g; Protein: 8g

88. Italian Sausage and Tortellini Soup

Preparation Time: 10 minutes
Cooking Time: 20 minutes
Servings: 6
Ingredients:

- 453g Italian sausage, casings removed
- 1 onion, chopped
- 2 cloves garlic, minced
- 946ml chicken broth
- 1 can (14 oz) diced tomatoes
- 1 package (9 oz) cheese tortellini
- 500g chopped spinach
- 7g Italian seasoning
- Salt and pepper to taste
- Grated Parmesan cheese (for serving)

Directions:
1. Preheat the Ninja Foodi Air Fryer to 190°C using the Air Fry function.
2. Cook Italian sausage in the Air Fryer basket until browned and cooked through.
3. Add chopped onion and minced garlic to the Air Fryer basket. Cook until softened.
4. Pour in chicken broth, diced tomatoes (with juices), cheese tortellini, chopped spinach, Italian seasoning, salt, and pepper.
5. Stir to combine all ingredients.
6. Air fry for 15-20 minutes until the tortellini are cooked and the soup is heated through.
7. Serve hot, garnished with grated Parmesan cheese.

Nutrition: Calories: 280kcal; Fat: 12g; Carb: 25g; Protein: 15g

89. Chicken and Broccoli Rice Casserole

Preparation Time: 15 minutes
Cooking Time: 25 minutes
Servings: 4
Ingredients:

- 453g chicken breast, cubed
- 240g white rice, uncooked
- 500ml chicken broth
- 500g broccoli florets
- 240g shredded cheddar cheese
- 120g sour cream
- 60g mayonnaise
- 15ml olive oil
- 2 cloves garlic, minced
- Salt and pepper to taste

Directions:
1. Preheat the Ninja Foodi Air Fryer to 190°C using the Air Fry function.
2. In the Air Fryer basket, combine cubed chicken breast, olive oil, minced garlic, salt, and pepper.
3. Air fry for 10-12 minutes until the chicken is cooked through.
4. Remove the Air Fryer basket and set aside the cooked chicken.
5. In the same Air Fryer basket, add white rice and chicken broth.
6. Air fry for 10 minutes, stirring halfway through.
7. Add broccoli florets to the Air Fryer basket. Air fry for an additional 5 minutes until the rice is cooked and the broccoli is tender.
8. Stir in cooked chicken, shredded cheddar cheese, sour cream, and mayonnaise until well combined.
9. Air fry for another 5 minutes until the cheese is melted and bubbly.
10. Serve hot.

Nutrition: Calories: 380kcal; Fat: 20g; Carb: 25g; Protein: 30g

90. Lemon Garlic Butter Shrimp and Asparagus

Preparation Time: 10 minutes
Cooking Time: 15 minutes
Servings: 4
Ingredients:

- 453g shrimp, peeled and deveined
- 1 bunch asparagus, trimmed

- 60g unsalted butter, melted
- 4 cloves garlic, minced
- Zest of 1 lemon
- Juice of 1 lemon
- Salt and pepper to taste
- Chopped fresh parsley (for garnish)

Directions:
1. Preheat the Ninja Foodi Air Fryer to 190°C using the Air Fry function.
2. In a bowl, combine peeled and deveined shrimp, trimmed asparagus, melted butter, minced garlic, lemon zest, lemon juice, salt, and pepper.
3. Toss until well coated.
4. Spread the shrimp and asparagus mixture in a single layer in the Air Fryer basket.
5. Air fry for 10-12 minutes, shaking halfway through, until the shrimp is pink and cooked through, and the asparagus is tender.
6. Serve hot, garnished with chopped fresh parsley.

Nutrition: Calories: 280kcal; Fat: 15g; Carb: 10g; Protein: 25g

Chapter 7. Desserts

91. Decadent Chocolate Lava Cake

Preparation Time: 10 minutes
Cooking Time: 12 minutes
Servings: 4
Ingredients:

- 120g dark chocolate chips
- 60g unsalted butter
- 60g granulated sugar
- 2 large eggs
- 7ml vanilla extract
- 30g all-purpose flour
- Powdered sugar (for dusting)
- Vanilla ice cream (optional, for serving)

Directions:

1. Preheat the Ninja Foodi Air Fryer to 175°C using the Air Fry function.
2. In a microwave-safe bowl, melt the dark chocolate chips and unsalted butter together until smooth.
3. In a separate bowl, whisk together granulated sugar, eggs, and vanilla extract until well combined.
4. Gradually pour the melted chocolate mixture into the egg mixture, stirring constantly.
5. Fold in all-purpose flour until just combined.
6. Divide the batter evenly among 4 ramekins.
7. Place the ramekins in the Air Fryer basket.
8. Air fry for 10-12 minutes until the edges are set but the center is still soft.
9. Remove from the Air Fryer and let them cool for a few minutes.
10. Dust with powdered sugar and serve warm, optionally with a scoop of vanilla ice cream.

Nutrition: Calories: 320kcal; Fat: 20g; Carb: 30g; Protein: 5g

92. Apple Crisp

Preparation Time: 15 minutes
Cooking Time: 20 minutes
Servings: 4
Ingredients:

- 4 medium apples, peeled and sliced
- 120g rolled oats
- 60g all-purpose flour
- 60g brown sugar
- 60g unsalted butter, melted
- 7g ground cinnamon
- 1.42g ground nutmeg
- Vanilla ice cream (optional, for serving)

Directions:
1. Preheat the Ninja Foodi Air Fryer to 190°C using the Air Fry function.
2. In a bowl, combine rolled oats, all-purpose flour, brown sugar, melted unsalted butter, ground cinnamon, and ground nutmeg. Mix until crumbly.
3. Place sliced apples in the Air Fryer basket.
4. Sprinkle the oat mixture evenly over the apples.
5. Air fry for 15-20 minutes until the topping is golden brown and the apples are tender.
6. Serve warm, optionally with a scoop of vanilla ice cream.

Nutrition: Calories: 280kcal; Fat: 10g; Carb: 48g; Protein: 3g

93. Vanilla Bean Cheesecake

Preparation Time: 20 minutes
Cooking Time: 35 minutes
Servings: 8
Ingredients:

- 240g graham cracker crumbs
- 30g granulated sugar
- 60g unsalted butter, melted
- 16 oz cream cheese, softened
- 120g granulated sugar
- 2 large eggs
- 60g sour cream
- 15g all-purpose flour
- 7ml vanilla extract
- Seeds from 1 vanilla bean (optional)
- Whipped cream (optional, for serving)

Directions:
1. Preheat the Ninja Foodi Air Fryer to 150°C using the Bake function.

2. In a bowl, mix together graham cracker crumbs, granulated sugar, and melted unsalted butter until well combined.
3. Press the crumb mixture firmly into the bottom of a 7-inch springform pan.
4. In another bowl, beat cream cheese and granulated sugar until smooth.
5. Add eggs, one at a time, beating well after each addition.
6. Beat in sour cream, all-purpose flour, vanilla extract, and vanilla bean seeds until well combined.
7. Pour the cream cheese mixture over the prepared crust.
8. Place the springform pan in the Air Fryer basket.
9. Bake for 30-35 minutes until the edges are set but the center is slightly wobbly.
10. Turn off the Air Fryer and let the cheesecake cool in the Air Fryer with the door slightly ajar.
11. Once cooled, refrigerate the cheesecake for at least 4 hours or overnight.
12. Serve chilled, optionally with whipped cream.

Nutrition: Calories: 380kcal; Fat: 28g; Carb: 28g; Protein: 7g

94. Mixed Berry Cobbler

Preparation Time: 15 minutes
Cooking Time: 25 minutes
Servings: 6
Ingredients:

- 500g mixed berries (such as strawberries, blueberries, raspberries)
- 60g granulated sugar
- 15ml lemon juice
- 240g all-purpose flour
- 120g granulated sugar
- 7g baking powder
- 1.42g salt
- 120g unsalted butter, melted
- Vanilla ice cream (optional, for serving)

Directions:
1. Preheat the Ninja Foodi Air Fryer to 190°C using the Air Fry function.
2. In a bowl, toss mixed berries with granulated sugar and lemon juice until well coated.
3. Transfer the berry mixture to a baking dish.
4. In another bowl, whisk together all-purpose flour, granulated sugar, baking powder, and salt.
5. Stir in melted unsalted butter until crumbly.
6. Sprinkle the crumb mixture evenly over the berries in the baking dish.
7. Place the baking dish in the Air Fryer basket.
8. Air fry for 20-25 minutes until the topping is golden brown and the berries are bubbling.

9. Serve warm, optionally with a scoop of vanilla ice cream.

Nutrition: Calories: 280kcal; Fat: 12g; Carb: 40g; Protein: 3g

95. Cinnamon Sugar Donuts

Preparation Time: 15 minutes

Cooking Time: 10 minutes

Servings: 6

Ingredients:

- 1 can (16.3 oz) refrigerated biscuits (8 count)
- 60g granulated sugar
- 15g ground cinnamon
- 60g unsalted butter, melted

Directions:

1. Preheat the Ninja Foodi Air Fryer to 175°C using the Air Fry function.
2. Remove the biscuits from the can and separate them.
3. Use a small round cookie cutter to cut out the center of each biscuit to form donuts.
4. In a shallow bowl, mix together granulated sugar and ground cinnamon.
5. Dip each donut into melted unsalted butter, then coat it with the cinnamon sugar mixture.
6. Place the coated donuts in the Air Fryer basket in a single layer.
7. Air fry for 5 minutes, then flip the donuts and air fry for an additional 5 minutes until golden brown.
8. Remove from the Air Fryer and let them cool slightly before serving.

Nutrition: Calories: 220kcal; Fat: 12g; Carb: 26g; Protein: 2g

96. Classic Tiramisu

Preparation Time: 20 minutes

Servings: 6

Ingredients:

- 240ml brewed espresso or strong coffee, cooled
- 30ml coffee liqueur (optional)
- 24 ladyfinger cookies
- 8 oz mascarpone cheese, softened
- 120g powdered sugar
- 7ml vanilla extract
- Cocoa powder, for dusting

Directions:

1. In a shallow dish, combine brewed espresso and coffee liqueur (if using).
2. Dip each ladyfinger cookie into the espresso mixture, soaking them briefly.

3. Arrange a layer of soaked ladyfingers in the bottom of a serving dish.
4. In a mixing bowl, beat mascarpone cheese, powdered sugar, and vanilla extract until smooth.
5. Spread half of the mascarpone mixture over the layer of ladyfingers.
6. Repeat with another layer of soaked ladyfingers and the remaining mascarpone mixture.
7. Cover and refrigerate the tiramisu for at least 4 hours or overnight.
8. Before serving, dust the top with cocoa powder.

Nutrition: Calories: 280kcal; Fat: 18g; Carb: 23g; Protein: 6g

97. Lemon Bars

Preparation Time: 15 minutes
Cooking Time: 20 minutes
Servings: 9
Ingredients:

- 240g all-purpose flour
- 120g powdered sugar, plus extra for dusting
- 120g unsalted butter, softened
- 2 large eggs
- 240g granulated sugar
- 30g all-purpose flour
- 1.42g baking powder
- 60ml lemon juice
- Zest of 1 lemon

Directions:
1. Preheat the Ninja Foodi Air Fryer to 175°C using the Bake function.
2. In a mixing bowl, combine 240g all-purpose flour, 120g powdered sugar, and softened unsalted butter. Mix until crumbly.
3. Press the mixture into the bottom of a greased 8x8-inch baking dish.
4. Bake in the preheated Air Fryer for 15 minutes until lightly golden.
5. In another bowl, beat eggs, granulated sugar, 30g all-purpose flour, baking powder, lemon juice, and lemon zest until well combined.
6. Pour the lemon mixture over the baked crust.
7. Return the baking dish to the Air Fryer and bake for an additional 20-25 minutes until set.
8. Let the lemon bars cool completely, then refrigerate for at least 2 hours before serving.
9. Dust with powdered sugar before serving and cut into squares.

Nutrition: Calories: 280kcal; Fat: 12g; Carb: 40g; Protein: 3g

98. Chocolate Chip Cookies

Preparation Time: 15 minutes
Cooking Time: 10 minutes
Servings: 12
Ingredients:

- 120g unsalted butter, softened
- 120g granulated sugar
- 60g packed brown sugar
- 1 large egg
- 7ml vanilla extract
- 370g all-purpose flour
- 3.5g baking soda
- 1.42g salt
- 240g semisweet chocolate chips

Directions:

1. Preheat the Ninja Foodi Air Fryer to 175°C using the Bake function.
2. In a mixing bowl, cream together softened unsalted butter, granulated sugar, and brown sugar until light and fluffy.
3. Beat in egg and vanilla extract until well combined.
4. In another bowl, whisk together all-purpose flour, baking soda, and salt.
5. Gradually add the dry ingredients to the wet ingredients, mixing until just combined.
6. Fold in semisweet chocolate chips.
7. Drop spoonfuls of cookie dough onto a greased Air Fryer basket, leaving space between each cookie.
8. Bake in the preheated Air Fryer for 8-10 minutes until the edges are golden brown.
9. Let the cookies cool on the Air Fryer tray before transferring to a wire rack to cool completely.

Nutrition: Calories: 210kcal; Fat: 11g; Carb: 28g; Protein: 2g

99. Blueberry Pie

Preparation Time: 20 minutes
Cooking Time: 30 minutes
Servings: 6
Ingredients:

- 1 9-inch refrigerated pie crust
- 946g fresh blueberries
- 120g granulated sugar

- 30g cornstarch
- 15ml lemon juice
- 3.5g ground cinnamon
- 1.42g salt
- 15g unsalted butter, diced
- 1 egg, beaten (for egg wash)
- 15g turbinado sugar (for sprinkling)

Directions:
1. Preheat the Ninja Foodi Air Fryer to 190°C using the Air Fry function.
2. Roll out the pie crust and fit it into a 9-inch pie dish, trimming any excess dough.
3. In a large bowl, mix together fresh blueberries, granulated sugar, cornstarch, lemon juice, ground cinnamon, and salt until well combined.
4. Pour the blueberry mixture into the prepared pie crust.
5. Dot the top of the blueberry filling with diced unsalted butter.
6. Place the pie dish in the Air Fryer basket.
7. Brush the edges of the pie crust with beaten egg and sprinkle turbinado sugar over the top.
8. Air fry for 25-30 minutes until the crust is golden brown and the filling is bubbly.
9. Remove from the Air Fryer and let the pie cool before slicing and serving.

Nutrition: Calories: 280kcal; Fat: 10g; Carb: 48g; Protein: 3g

100. Raspberry Swirl Brownies

Preparation Time: 15 minutes
Cooking Time: 25 minutes
Servings: 9
Ingredients:

- 120g unsalted butter
- 120g semisweet chocolate chips
- 240g granulated sugar
- 2 large eggs
- 7ml vanilla extract
- 150g all-purpose flour
- 60g unsweetened cocoa powder
- 1.42g salt
- 120g raspberry jam

Directions:
1. Preheat the Ninja Foodi Air Fryer to 175°C using the Bake function.
2. In a microwave-safe bowl, melt unsalted butter and semisweet chocolate chips together until smooth.

3. In a mixing bowl, whisk together granulated sugar, eggs, and vanilla extract until well combined.
4. Gradually add the melted chocolate mixture to the egg mixture, stirring constantly.
5. In another bowl, sift together all-purpose flour, cocoa powder, and salt.
6. Gradually add the dry ingredients to the wet ingredients, mixing until just combined.
7. Pour the brownie batter into a greased 8x8-inch baking dish, spreading it evenly.
8. Drop spoonfuls of raspberry jam onto the brownie batter. Use a knife to swirl the jam into the batter.
9. Place the baking dish in the Air Fryer basket.
10. Bake for 20-25 minutes until the edges are set but the center is still slightly soft.
11. Let the brownies cool completely before slicing and serving.

Nutrition: Calories: 280kcal; Fat: 14g; Carb: 38g; Protein: 3g

101. Peach Crumble

Preparation Time: 15 minutes
Cooking Time: 20 minutes
Servings: 6
Ingredients:

- 946g sliced peaches (fresh or canned, drained)
- 60g granulated sugar
- 15ml lemon juice
- 3.5g ground cinnamon
- 1.42g ground nutmeg
- 240g old-fashioned oats
- 120g all-purpose flour
- 120g packed brown sugar
- 60g unsalted butter, melted

Directions:
1. Preheat the Ninja Foodi Air Fryer to 190°C using the Air Fry function.
2. In a large bowl, toss together sliced peaches, granulated sugar, lemon juice, ground cinnamon, and ground nutmeg until well coated.
3. Transfer the peach mixture to a greased baking dish.
4. In another bowl, combine old-fashioned oats, all-purpose flour, packed brown sugar, and melted unsalted butter. Mix until crumbly.
5. Sprinkle the oat mixture evenly over the peach mixture in the baking dish.
6. Place the baking dish in the Air Fryer basket.
7. Air fry for 15-20 minutes until the topping is golden brown and the peaches are bubbling.
8. Remove from the Air Fryer and let the crumble cool slightly before serving.

Nutrition: Calories: 280kcal; Fat: 10g; Carb: 40g; Protein: 8g

102. Key Lime Pie

Preparation Time: 20 minutes

Cooking Time: 30 minutes

Servings: 8

Ingredients:

- 1 9-inch prepared graham cracker crust
- 3 large eggs, separated
- 1 can (14 oz) sweetened condensed milk
- 120ml key lime juice
- 15g lime zest
- Whipped cream (for serving)

Directions:

1. Preheat the Ninja Foodi Air Fryer to 175°C using the Bake function.
2. In a mixing bowl, beat egg yolks until thick and lemon-colored.
3. Gradually beat in sweetened condensed milk, key lime juice, and lime zest until well combined.
4. In another bowl, beat egg whites until stiff peaks form.
5. Gently fold beaten egg whites into the lime mixture until just combined.
6. Pour the lime mixture into the prepared graham cracker crust.
7. Place the pie dish in the Air Fryer basket.
8. Bake for 25-30 minutes until the filling is set and the edges are golden brown.
9. Remove from the Air Fryer and let the pie cool completely.
10. Refrigerate for at least 4 hours before serving.
11. Serve chilled, topped with whipped cream.

Nutrition: Calories: 320kcal; Fat: 12g; Carb: 45g; Protein: 7g

103. Banoffee Pie

Preparation Time: 20 minutes

Servings: 8

Ingredients:

- 1 9-inch prepared graham cracker crust
- 3 ripe bananas, sliced
- 1 can (14 oz) sweetened condensed milk
- 30g unsalted butter
- 60g packed brown sugar
- 240g heavy cream

- 7ml vanilla extract
- Chocolate shavings (for garnish)

Directions:
1. Preheat the Ninja Foodi Air Fryer to 175°C using the Bake function.
2. In a saucepan, place the unopened can of sweetened condensed milk and cover it with water. Bring the water to a simmer and let it cook for 3 hours, adding more water as needed to keep the can submerged.
3. After 3 hours, carefully remove the can from the water and let it cool completely.
4. Open the can and spread the caramelized condensed milk (dulce de leche) over the bottom of the prepared graham cracker crust.
5. Arrange sliced bananas over the caramel layer.
6. In a skillet, melt unsalted butter over medium heat. Add packed brown sugar and cook, stirring constantly, until the sugar has dissolved and the mixture is bubbly.
7. Pour the butter-sugar mixture over the bananas in the pie crust.
8. In a mixing bowl, beat heavy cream and vanilla extract until stiff peaks form.
9. Spread whipped cream over the pie, covering the banana layer completely.
10. Chill the pie in the refrigerator for at least 4 hours or overnight.
11. Before serving, garnish with chocolate shavings.

Nutrition: Calories: 380kcal; Fat: 22g; Carb: 45g; Protein: 4g

104. Red Velvet Cupcakes

Preparation Time: 20 minutes
Cooking Time: 15 minutes
Servings: 12
Ingredients:

- 370g all-purpose flour
- 120g granulated sugar
- 60g unsweetened cocoa powder
- 3.5g baking soda
- 3.5g salt
- 120g unsalted butter, softened
- 2 large eggs
- 120ml buttermilk
- 15g red food coloring
- 7ml vanilla extract
- 7ml white vinegar
- Cream cheese frosting (store-bought or homemade)

- Red velvet cake crumbs (for garnish, optional)

Directions:
1. Preheat the Ninja Foodi Air Fryer to 175°C using the Bake function.
2. In a bowl, sift together all-purpose flour, granulated sugar, cocoa powder, baking soda, and salt.
3. In another bowl, beat softened unsalted butter and eggs until creamy.
4. Gradually add buttermilk, red food coloring, vanilla extract, and white vinegar, mixing until well combined.
5. Gradually add the dry ingredients to the wet ingredients, mixing until smooth.
6. Line a muffin tin with cupcake liners.
7. Fill each cupcake liner about 2/3 full with the red velvet batter.
8. Place the muffin tin in the Air Fryer basket.
9. Air fry for 12-15 minutes until a toothpick inserted into the center comes out clean.
10. Remove the cupcakes from the Air Fryer and let them cool completely.
11. Once cooled, frost the cupcakes with cream cheese frosting and garnish with red velvet cake crumbs if desired.

Nutrition: Calories: 180kcal; Fat: 18; Carb: 24g; Protein: 3g

105. Chocolate Covered Strawberries

Preparation Time: 15 minutes
Cooking Time: 30 minutes
Servings: 12
Ingredients:

- 12 large strawberries, washed and dried
- 240g semisweet chocolate chips
- 15ml coconut oil
- Assorted toppings (chopped nuts, shredded coconut, sprinkles)

Directions:
1. Preheat the Ninja Foodi Air Fryer to 175°C using the Air Fry function.
2. In a microwave-safe bowl, combine semisweet chocolate chips and coconut oil.
3. Microwave in 30-second intervals, stirring between each interval, until the chocolate is completely melted and smooth.
4. Dip each strawberry into the melted chocolate, allowing any excess to drip off.
5. Place the chocolate-covered strawberries on a parchment-lined tray.
6. Immediately sprinkle your desired toppings over the chocolate before it sets.
7. Place the tray in the refrigerator for about 30 minutes to allow the chocolate to set.
8. Once the chocolate is firm, serve and enjoy!

Nutrition: Calories: 70kcal; Fat: 5g; Carb: 7g; Protein: 1g

106. Strawberry Shortcake

Preparation Time: 20 minutes
Cooking Time: 10 minutes
Servings: 6
Ingredients:

- 370g all-purpose flour
- 60g granulated sugar
- 15g baking powder
- 1.42g salt
- 6 tablespoons unsalted butter, cold and cubed
- 120ml milk
- 7ml vanilla extract
- 500g sliced strawberries
- 30g granulated sugar
- Whipped cream

Directions:
1. Preheat the Ninja Foodi Air Fryer to 175°C using the Bake function.
2. In a bowl, whisk together all-purpose flour, granulated sugar, baking powder, and salt.
3. Cut in cold cubed unsalted butter until the mixture resembles coarse crumbs.
4. Stir in milk and vanilla extract until just combined.
5. Drop spoonfuls of dough onto a greased Air Fryer basket to form biscuits.
6. Air fry for 8-10 minutes until golden brown and cooked through.
7. In another bowl, toss sliced strawberries with granulated sugar and let them macerate for a few minutes.
8. To serve, split the biscuits in half, top with macerated strawberries, and whipped cream.

Nutrition: Calories: 280kcal; Fat: 12g; Carb: 38g; Protein: 4g

107. Chocolate Mousse

Preparation Time: 20 minutes
Cooking Time: 4 hours
Servings: 4
Ingredients:

- 6 oz semisweet chocolate, chopped
- 30g unsalted butter
- 3 large eggs, separated
- 60g granulated sugar

- 240g heavy cream
- 7ml vanilla extract
- Chocolate shavings (for garnish, optional)

Directions:
1. In a microwave-safe bowl, melt semisweet chocolate and unsalted butter together until smooth. Let it cool slightly.
2. In a separate bowl, beat egg yolks and granulated sugar until pale and thick.
3. Gradually whisk in melted chocolate mixture until well combined.
4. In another bowl, beat egg whites until stiff peaks form.
5. Gently fold beaten egg whites into the chocolate mixture until no white streaks remain.
6. In another bowl, whip heavy cream and vanilla extract until stiff peaks form.
7. Gently fold whipped cream into the chocolate mixture until smooth and well combined.
8. Spoon the chocolate mousse into serving glasses or bowls.
9. Chill in the refrigerator for at least 4 hours or until set.
10. Garnish with chocolate shavings before serving.

Nutrition: Calories: 430kcal; Fat: 34g; Carb: 28g; Protein: 6g

108. Lemon Meringue Pie

Preparation Time: 30 minutes
Cooking Time: 15 minutes
Servings: 8
Ingredients:

- 1 9-inch prepared graham cracker crust
- 370g granulated sugar
- 60g cornstarch
- 1.42g salt
- 400ml water
- 3 large egg yolks
- 15g lemon zest
- 120ml fresh lemon juice
- 30g unsalted butter
- 4 large egg whites
- 1.42g cream of tartar
- 120g granulated sugar

Directions:
1. Preheat the Ninja Foodi Air Fryer to 175°C using the Bake function.
2. In a saucepan, whisk together granulated sugar, cornstarch, and salt.

3. Gradually whisk in water until smooth.
4. Cook over medium heat, stirring constantly, until the mixture thickens and boils.
5. Boil for 1 minute, then remove from heat.
6. In a small bowl, beat egg yolks slightly.
7. Gradually whisk about 1 cup of the hot mixture into the beaten egg yolks.
8. Return the egg yolk mixture to the saucepan and bring to a boil.
9. Boil for 1 minute, stirring constantly.
10. Remove from heat and stir in lemon zest, lemon juice, and unsalted butter until well combined.
11. Pour the lemon mixture into the prepared graham cracker crust.
12. In a mixing bowl, beat egg whites and cream of tartar until foamy.
13. Gradually add granulated sugar, beating until stiff peaks form.
14. Spread the meringue over the hot filling, sealing the edges to the crust.
15. Bake in the preheated Air Fryer for 12-15 minutes until the meringue is golden brown.
16. Cool on a wire rack for 1 hour, then refrigerate for at least 4 hours before serving.

Nutrition: Calories: 320kcal; Fat: 11g; Carb: 52g; Protein: 4g

Chapter 8. Homemade Sauces and Dips

109. Classic Marinara Sauce

Preparation Time: 10 minutes
Cooking Time: 20 minutes
Servings: Makes about 500g
Ingredients:

- 30ml olive oil
- 1 small onion, finely chopped
- 2 cloves garlic, minced
- 1 can (28 oz) crushed tomatoes
- 7g dried oregano
- 7g dried basil
- 3.5g salt
- 1.42g black pepper
- 15g tomato paste
- 7g sugar (optional)

Directions:
1. Preheat the Ninja Foodi Air Fryer using the Sauté function. Add olive oil, chopped onion, and minced garlic. Sauté until onions are translucent, about 3-4 minutes.
2. Add crushed tomatoes, dried oregano, dried basil, salt, black pepper, tomato paste, and sugar (if using). Stir well to combine.
3. Close the lid of the Ninja Foodi and select the Air Fryer function. Set the temperature to 175°C and the timer to 20 minutes.
4. After 10 minutes, open the lid and stir the sauce to prevent sticking.
5. Once done, adjust seasoning if needed.
6. Serve hot with pasta or use as a pizza sauce. Store any leftovers in an airtight container in the refrigerator for up to 5 days.

Nutrition: Calories: 50kcal; Fat: 3g; Carb: 6g; Protein: 1g

110. Creamy Garlic Aioli

Preparation Time: 5 minutes

Cooking Time: 5 minutes
Servings: Makes about 120g
Ingredients:

- 120g mayonnaise
- 2 cloves garlic, minced
- 15ml lemon juice
- Salt and pepper to taste

Directions:

1. In a bowl, combine mayonnaise, minced garlic, and lemon juice.
2. Mix well until smooth and creamy.
3. Season with salt and pepper to taste.
4. Serve immediately or refrigerate until ready to use.
5. Enjoy as a dip for fries, veggies, or spread on sandwiches and burgers.

Nutrition: Calories: 100kcal; Fat: 11g; Carb: 0g; Protein: 0g

111. Tangy Barbecue Sauce

Preparation Time: 5 minutes
Cooking Time: 10 minutes
Servings: Makes about 1 1/500g
Ingredients:

- 240g ketchup
- 60ml apple cider vinegar
- 30g brown sugar
- 15ml Worcestershire sauce
- 7g smoked paprika
- 3.5g garlic powder
- 3.5g onion powder
- 1.42g salt
- 1.42g black pepper

Directions:

1. In a bowl, whisk together all ingredients until well combined.
2. Transfer the mixture to the Ninja Foodi Air Fryer basket.
3. Select the Air Fry function and set the temperature to 175°C and the timer to 10 minutes.
4. Stir the sauce halfway through the cooking time.
5. Once done, let the sauce cool before transferring it to a jar.
6. Use immediately or store in the refrigerator for up to 2 weeks.

Nutrition: Calories: 50kcal; Fat: 0g; Carb: 13g; Protein: 0g

112. Chunky Salsa

Preparation Time: 10 minutes

Servings: Makes about 500g

Ingredients:

- 4 ripe tomatoes, diced
- 1 small red onion, finely chopped
- 1 jalapeño pepper, seeded and finely chopped
- 60g fresh cilantro, chopped
- 2 cloves garlic, minced
- 30ml lime juice
- 3.5g salt
- 1.42g black pepper

Directions:

1. In a bowl, combine diced tomatoes, chopped red onion, chopped jalapeño pepper, minced garlic, chopped cilantro, lime juice, salt, and black pepper.
2. Mix well to combine all the ingredients.
3. Transfer the salsa mixture to the Ninja Foodi Air Fryer basket.
4. Select the Air Fry function and set the temperature to 175°C and the timer to 5 minutes.
5. After 5 minutes, open the Air Fryer and stir the salsa.
6. Continue air frying for another 5 minutes until the salsa is slightly charred and flavors are well combined.
7. Remove from the Air Fryer and let it cool slightly before serving.
8. Serve with tortilla chips or as a topping for tacos, burritos, or grilled meats.

Nutrition: Calories: 15kcal; Fat: 0g; Carb: 3g; Protein: 1g

113. Honey Mustard Dip

Preparation Time: 5 minutes

Cooking Time: 5 minutes

Servings: Makes about 120g

Ingredients:

- 60g mayonnaise
- 30g Dijon mustard
- 15ml honey
- 7ml lemon juice
- Salt and pepper to taste

Directions:

1. In a bowl, whisk together mayonnaise, Dijon mustard, honey, and lemon juice until smooth.
2. Season with salt and pepper to taste.
3. Transfer the honey mustard dip to a serving bowl.
4. Serve immediately or refrigerate until ready to use.
5. Enjoy as a dip for chicken tenders, pretzels, or veggies.

Nutrition: Calories: 60kcal; Fat: 5g; Carb: 4g; Protein: 0g

114. Basil Pesto

Preparation Time: 10 minutes
Cooking Time: 5 minutes
Servings: Makes about 240g
Ingredients:

- 500g fresh basil leaves, packed
- 60g pine nuts or walnuts
- 2 cloves garlic, minced
- 120g grated Parmesan cheese
- 60ml olive oil
- Salt and pepper to taste

Directions:
1. In the bowl of a food processor, combine basil leaves, pine nuts or walnuts, minced garlic, and grated Parmesan cheese.
2. Pulse until finely chopped.
3. With the food processor running, gradually add olive oil in a steady stream until the pesto reaches your desired consistency.
4. Season with salt and pepper to taste.
5. Transfer the basil pesto to a jar or airtight container.
6. Serve immediately or refrigerate for later use.
7. Enjoy tossed with pasta, spread on sandwiches, or as a dip for bread.

Nutrition: Calories: 150kcal; Fat: 15g; Carb: 2g; Protein: 3g

115. Chunky Salsa

Preparation Time: 10 minutes
Cooking Time: 10 minutes
Servings: Makes about 500g
Ingredients:

- 4 ripe tomatoes, diced
- 1 small red onion, finely chopped

- 1 jalapeño pepper, seeded and finely chopped
- 60g fresh cilantro, chopped
- 2 cloves garlic, minced
- 30ml lime juice
- 3.5g salt
- 1.42g black pepper

Directions:
1. In a bowl, combine diced tomatoes, chopped red onion, chopped jalapeño pepper, minced garlic, chopped cilantro, lime juice, salt, and black pepper.
2. Mix well to combine all the ingredients.
3. Transfer the salsa mixture to the Ninja Foodi Air Fryer basket.
4. Select the Air Fry function and set the temperature to 175°C and the timer to 5 minutes.
5. After 5 minutes, open the Air Fryer and stir the salsa.
6. Continue air frying for another 5 minutes until the salsa is slightly charred and flavors are well combined.
7. Remove from the Air Fryer and let it cool slightly before serving.
8. Serve with tortilla chips or as a topping for tacos, burritos, or grilled meats.

Nutrition: Calories: 15kcal; Fat: 0g; Carb: 3g; Protein: 1g

116. Honey Mustard Dip

Preparation Time: 5 minutes
Cooking Time: 0 minutes
Servings: Makes about 120g
Ingredients:

- 60g mayonnaise
- 30g Dijon mustard
- 15ml honey
- 7ml lemon juice
- Salt and pepper to taste

Directions:
1. In a bowl, whisk together mayonnaise, Dijon mustard, honey, and lemon juice until smooth.
2. Season with salt and pepper to taste.
3. Transfer the honey mustard dip to a serving bowl.
4. Serve immediately or refrigerate until ready to use.
5. Enjoy as a dip for chicken tenders, pretzels, or veggies.

Nutrition: Calories: 60kcal; Fat: 5g; Carb: 4g; Protein: 0g

117. Basil Pesto

Preparation Time: 10 minutes
Cooking Time: 0 minutes
Servings: Makes about 240g
Ingredients:

- 500g fresh basil leaves, packed
- 60g pine nuts or walnuts
- 2 cloves garlic, minced
- 120g grated Parmesan cheese
- 60ml olive oil
- Salt and pepper to taste

Directions:
1. In the bowl of a food processor, combine basil leaves, pine nuts or walnuts, minced garlic, and grated Parmesan cheese.
2. Pulse until finely chopped.
3. With the food processor running, gradually add olive oil in a steady stream until the pesto reaches your desired consistency.
4. Season with salt and pepper to taste.
5. Transfer the basil pesto to a jar or airtight container.
6. Serve immediately or refrigerate for later use.
7. Enjoy tossed with pasta, spread on sandwiches, or as a dip for bread.

Nutrition: Calories: 150kcal; Fat: 15g; Carb: 2g; Protein: 3g

118. Teriyaki Sauce

Preparation Time: 5 minutes
Cooking Time: 10 minutes
Servings: Makes about 1 cup
Ingredients:

- 120ml soy sauce
- 60ml water
- 30g brown sugar
- 15ml honey
- 2 cloves garlic, minced
- 7g grated fresh ginger
- 15g cornstarch
- 30ml water

Directions:
1. In a small saucepan, combine soy sauce, water, brown sugar, honey, minced garlic, and grated ginger.
2. Bring the mixture to a simmer over medium heat, stirring occasionally.
3. In a small bowl, mix cornstarch and water until smooth to make a slurry.
4. Gradually add the cornstarch slurry to the simmering sauce, stirring constantly until the sauce thickens.
5. Continue to cook for another 2-3 minutes until the sauce reaches the desired consistency.
6. Remove from heat and let it cool slightly before serving.
7. Serve as a dipping sauce for chicken, beef, or vegetables, or use as a glaze for grilled meats.

Nutrition: Calories: 40kcal; Fat: 0g; Carb: 10g; Protein: 1g

119. Ranch Dressing

Preparation Time: 5 minutes
Cooking Time: 0 minutes
Servings: Makes about 240g
Ingredients:

- 120g mayonnaise
- 120g sour cream
- 60ml buttermilk
- 15g chopped fresh chives
- 15g chopped fresh parsley
- 7g dried dill
- 3.5g garlic powder
- 3.5g onion powder
- Salt and pepper to taste

Directions:
1. In a bowl, whisk together mayonnaise, sour cream, and buttermilk until smooth.
2. Stir in chopped fresh chives, chopped fresh parsley, dried dill, garlic powder, onion powder, salt, and pepper.
3. Mix until well combined and creamy.
4. Taste and adjust seasoning if necessary.
5. Transfer the ranch dressing to a jar or airtight container.
6. Serve immediately or refrigerate for at least 1 hour to allow the flavors to meld.
7. Enjoy as a dressing for salads, dipping sauce for veggies, or drizzle over baked potatoes.

Nutrition: Calories: 110kcal; Fat: 11g; Carb: 1g; Protein: 1g

120. Guacamole

Preparation Time: 10 minutes

Cooking Time: 0 minutes
Servings: Makes about 500g
Ingredients:

- 2 ripe avocados
- 1 small tomato, diced
- 60g diced red onion
- 1 jalapeño pepper, seeded and finely chopped
- 1 clove garlic, minced
- 30g chopped fresh cilantro
- 15ml lime juice
- Salt and pepper to taste

Directions:
1. Cut the avocados in half, remove the pits, and scoop the flesh into a bowl.
2. Mash the avocados with a fork until smooth or leave chunky if desired.
3. Add diced tomato, diced red onion, finely chopped jalapeño pepper, minced garlic, chopped fresh cilantro, and lime juice to the mashed avocados.
4. Mix well to combine all the ingredients.
5. Season with salt and pepper to taste.
6. Serve immediately with tortilla chips or as a topping for tacos, nachos, or sandwiches.

Nutrition: Calories: 60kcal; Fat: 5g; Carb: 5g; Protein: 1g

Conclusion

In the culinary world, innovation is the key to evolution. The Ninja Foodi Air Fryer, with its revolutionary design and multifunctionality, has redefined the art of cooking. As we conclude this comprehensive book, it's evident that this appliance isn't just a kitchen gadget; it's a gateway to culinary mastery and healthier living.

Throughout this journey, we've explored the limitless possibilities offered by the Ninja Foodi Air Fryer. From crispy air-fried delights to succulent roasts and hearty stews, this appliance has empowered both novice and seasoned chefs to create restaurant-quality meals from the comfort of their own kitchens.

One of the most remarkable features of the Ninja Foodi Air Fryer is its versatility. It seamlessly transitions between air frying, roasting, baking, grilling, and dehydrating, offering a myriad of cooking options in a single appliance. This versatility not only saves time and counter space but also inspires culinary experimentation. Whether you're craving golden-brown fries, tender steaks, or delectable desserts, the Ninja Foodi Air Fryer has you covered.

Moreover, this book has served as a guide, offering a treasure trove of recipes, tips, and techniques to unleash the full potential of the Ninja Foodi Air Fryer. From classic comfort foods to exotic cuisines, each recipe has been carefully crafted to deliver mouthwatering results. Whether you're hosting a dinner party or preparing a quick weeknight meal, you'll find inspiration within these pages.

Beyond its culinary prowess, the Ninja Foodi Air Fryer embodies the spirit of healthy cooking. By using up to 75% less fat than traditional frying methods, it allows you to indulge in your favorite foods guilt-free. Whether you're air frying chicken wings or baking pastries, you can enjoy the crispy texture and delicious flavor without compromising on your health goals.

Furthermore, the Ninja Foodi Air Fryer promotes sustainability by reducing energy consumption and minimizing food waste. Its efficient design ensures even cooking and optimal results with minimal preheating time, saving both time and energy. Additionally, its large capacity allows you to cook multiple servings at once, making meal prep a breeze.

As we conclude our exploration of the Ninja Foodi Air Fryer, it's important to reflect on the impact it has had on the culinary landscape. By combining innovation, versatility, and health-consciousness, this appliance has revolutionized the way we cook and eat. It has empowered home cooks to unleash their creativity, experiment with new flavors, and embrace healthier cooking habits.

In closing, the Ninja Foodi Air Fryer isn't just a kitchen appliance; it's a culinary companion that unlocks a world of possibilities. Whether you're a novice cook or a seasoned chef, it has something to offer everyone. So, fire up your Ninja Foodi Air Fryer, embark on a culinary adventure, and discover the endless possibilities that await you in the kitchen. Happy cooking!

Printed in Great Britain
by Amazon